To Nick Roosevelt

with the friendship of

Hermann Hagedorn

1924.

ROOSEVELT
PROPHET OF UNITY

ROOSEVELT
PROPHET OF UNITY

BY

HERMANN HAGEDORN

CHARLES SCRIBNER'S SONS
NEW YORK · LONDON
1924

TO THOSE
WHO TAKE UP THE TORCH

ROOSEVELT
PROPHET OF UNITY

"TELL me about this man Roosevelt."
It was a European statesman of considerable
eminence who recently spoke the words to
the writer of these pages. "I have just returned from a trip across your country. I
have stopped at all the great cities between
the Atlantic and the Pacific, and wherever I
have been men have talked to me about
Roosevelt. I remember, of course, that there
was much interest in him in Europe when he
was President. But that is a long time ago,
and I have found men speaking of Roosevelt
as they speak of a living leader. What was
his power, what did he accomplish, that he
should be so vividly remembered?"

There is no better answer to the query of
this astonished minister of state than the
words, almost classic in their dignity, of an
old man living away from the world, high

up in the mountains of Colorado: "He was my friend and the friend of all humanity. He opened my eyes and put hope in my heart as no living man had ever done before. Being an ignorant man—without even a common-school education—I sought only for truth, and, by heaven, I found it in him."

Roosevelt opened men's eyes and put hope in men's hearts; he reinterpreted to them the democratic ideal; he made the dream of brotherhood for flashing instants a living possibility. *Strive for unity*, he pleaded; and strove mightily himself in a world of opposing aims and prejudices and passions to make that unity a reality.

I

IT has been said so often that the statement has come to be regarded as axiomatic, that it takes time to get the measure of a great man. Time is needed, men repeat, to mellow personal prejudice, to clarify obscure issues, to bring forward hidden facts, to enable the minds of a man's contemporaries to recover from the shock of the new point of view which he has presented, and to adjust themselves to the new standards which he has set up. Time is needed, we are told, to separate the achievements which were noteworthy or magnificent from the acts which merely made a noise; to separate the triumphs which were undramatic but lasting from the triumphs which were obvious but, in the long run, unimportant. Time is needed, above all, historians declare, to enable the discriminating intelligence to determine what effect a great man's career has had on his own generation and on the generations which succeed him, and to speculate what might have occurred, for good or ill, if the vision and power which he was had not thrust themselves across the tendencies of his age. The common phrase is that it takes perspective to judge any man who has created a distinguished commotion in his particular period.

It is a familiar saying that we have to get away from a mountain to be able ade-

quately to estimate its size; the higher the
mountain the farther we have to get away
from it. Washington, no doubt, looms
greater to-day than he did a century and a
quarter ago, because we are able to note now
the reverberations which his deeds caused in
the four corners of the globe. And yet
Washington's contemporaries, in the main,
were fully aware that a titan lived among
them. They did not know the exact dimen-
sions of the titan, just as the man at the foot
of a great height may not know or be able to
estimate the altitude of the snowy summit;
but they recognized that here was something
overwhelmingly majestic.

The same was true in a lesser degree of
Lincoln. Posterity has done little more than
affirm the estimate of the most deep-seeing
of Lincoln's own contemporaries. It did
not take the perspective of long years for
Lincoln's countrymen to get his measure. If
Lincoln has an added splendor in our eyes,
it is due to the reflection of the admiration
and awe of all civilized mankind, not to the

clearer vision of succeeding generations. It is only that to-day all the world sees what Walt Whitman and James Russell Lowell and thousands of others saw and expressed in great or simple words in 1865.

When a cool-headed and sagacious student of men and governments, the historian John Morley, observed twenty years ago that "the two most extraordinary things" he had seen in America had been "Niagara Falls and the President of the United States—both great wonders of nature," he gave expression to an intellectual reaction which a large number of Roosevelt's less articulate contemporaries had experienced. They were conscious that a great new force was active in their midst; that a personality which had been familiar to them for twenty years, a man they had seen emerge from the great mass and disappear, emerge again more powerful and more compelling and again disappear, had grown into a figure of huge proportions, which caught and held the attention and the imagination of the civilized world. They saw him challenge and subdue forces which had seemed invincible; they saw him take a party whose leadership was openly reactionary and make it for eight years an instrument of progress. Roosevelt's contemporaries—and best among them perhaps the unsophisticated and the unlearned—recognized that, like the contemporaries of Washington and Lincoln, they too were watching a titan in action.

Surely it does not require the passage of time to determine whether a man who has won the applause of his generation has those qualities of greatness which have, in the course of history, set men on pinnacles above the vast masses of their fellows; but it does unquestionably, however, take time to define the exact nature of that greatness. It is doubtful whether more than a few of those who saw Roosevelt at the height of his power, and believed in him, understood clearly what the powerful spirit to which they looked for leadership was seeking to achieve and was achieving and did achieve before the story was done. In that achievement the dramatic successes of his administration of public office were only incidents, and the most dramatic, perhaps, were in the end the least significant in the development of the action whose large outlines are only now beginning to be apparent.

It is five years since Roosevelt died; it is fifteen since he laid down the Presidency; it is forty-two since he first broke, a new, strange, bright-burning star, through the murky atmosphere of American political life. The generation which first acclaimed him and made room for his boyish, energetic figure on the seats of leadership, has completely passed from the scene; the next, which he dominated and enthralled, and led into unexplored regions and into battle after battle, with uneven fortune, is in the process of passing. A generation to whom Roosevelt at the height of his political power is at most only a glowing memory of youth, is assuming control. His followers are scattered under many stand-

ards. Even the stanchest upholder of the
ancient maxim may well agree that the time
has come when it is possible to define with
some measure of exactness the nature of the
service rendered by this extraordinary being
whose greatness his contemporaries instinctively felt and even the most critical of them
generously admitted.

He achieved notable success in many fields.
He was an authority on naval history at
twenty-three, an authority on the history of
of the westward march of American civilization ten years later. Naturalists of the first
rank recognized him as an acute and trust-
worthy observer of the fauna of three conti-
nents, who had contributed substantially to
the knowledge of wild life and had rendered
extraordinary service in its preservation. As
an explorer he achieved distinction, and in one
comparatively brief but extremely perilous
expedition won a place among the trail-
makers of the wilderness.

As a writer he had an unusual combination
of gifts. His narratives are lucid and swift,

his descriptions full of color and significant detail, his literary criticism straightforward and free from the jargon and the catchwords to which all but the masters of the art are too frequently subject, his political writings direct and clear, open to the most untutored intelligence and flashing at intervals with arresting and illuminating epithets. Under the stress of emotion, in some of the prefaces to his hunting books, in a descriptive passage here and there, in his appeal for imagination in the writing of history, and occasionally in the peroration of a public address, his prose became transmuted into the pure gold of poetry.

As an orator he was powerful and compelling; as a soldier he exhibited qualities of leadership which, combined with the qualities of foresight, courage, and resourcefulness which he unfolded in public office might, in a greater war, have put him in the company of the world's great generals. As a politician he was respected and feared by the astute political strategists of a period which was not lacking in brilliant manipulators of issues, assemblies, and individual interests and ambitions, winning his victories less by adroitness in handling other politicians than by his ability to place his case vividly before the minds of the people and to inspire them to accept his guidance. His faith in the people was as profound as Jefferson's; but it was more realistic. With the issues placed clearly before them, he believed that the people could be trusted to go right; left without intelligent guidance, he bluntly admitted, their voice was as likely to be the voice of the devil as the voice of God.

He was, as the man who was his Secretary of State has said, "an almost perfect executive," indefatigable, energetic, dignified, sympathetic; swift and generally wise in his decisions; discriminating in the appointment of his subordinates and willing to give them the widest possible measure of independence of action and more than the credit which was their due; always prepared for the next move, whether that move were his own or his opponents'; interested in every phase of governmental activity or social, economic, political, artistic, or religious life.

As head of the nation he achieved certain immediate triumphs at home and abroad that gave a glamour to his administration which deepens rather than fades as one after the other his successors pass across the scene, leaving their own records beside his. As a moral leader he had no equal in his time. He swept through the smoky air of American political life like a whirlwind, and into the filthy stalls of corruption like a flood.

He had magnificent gifts and he utilized them to the last ounce of power in the service of his countrymen. Taken in conjunction with his personal qualities, his strength, his tenderness, his courage, his humor, his charm, his unceasing consideration for others, his rare gift of giving and inspiring friendship, they constitute a personality in its warmth and its richness unique in American history and rare in the history of the world.

II

ROOSEVELT's many-sidedness was a source of amazement to all who came in contact with him. Naturalists found him at home not only on the main highroads of their science but on the bypaths which they imagined were familiar only to specialists; historians discovered that he had an astonishing reservoir of knowledge of the rise and fall of European civilizations; he could quote ancient German poetry one minute and ancient French the next, describe in detail the movements of obscure battles, come face to face with an Irishman in a line of handshakers and instantly recall that, fifteen years before, the man had won the world's high-jumping championship at such and such a place with such and such a jump. Such brilliant diversity of gifts intensifies the impression of greatness, but it does not make it easy for the observer even after an interval to define that greatness. It gives an aspect of complexity to a story which may at bottom not be complex at all; it evokes the examination of the great life by phases rather than as a whole; it dazzles and it blinds. In order that Roosevelt's greatness may be even approximately measured and the fundamental service which he rendered set in sharp relief, it is essential that his diverse gifts and the successes which crowned his persistent and skilful exercise of them should be seen in correct proportion. To suggest that he was as eminent in one field as in another is to be clearly unjust to his service in the field or fields in which he was supreme.

He wrote discriminating and vivid histories which have not been supplanted in the fields which they cover; but he would himself have protested with emphasis against the laudation which should attempt to place him on an equality with Parkman and Fiske. He was all his life an eager student of natural history, keenly interested in every new discovery and new theory which pertained to it; but by the nature of his activities he was not a scientist, in the strict sense, at all, but a brilliant amateur of science to whom scientific study was a form of recreation and scientific observation an incident of the adventure of hunting and of life in the open. He has a high place among naturalists, and history may yet say of him that he stands beside Audubon as an interpreter to the popular mind of the phenomena of the natural world; but he himself would have been the last to agree that his place was with Osborn and Merriam.

He was an assiduous, colorful, and occasionally a brilliant writer; but the critics, he complained early in his career, refused to regard either his hunting narratives or his historical works as literature, and, except possibly in the field of epistolary literature, in which his peculiar and individual distinction has been revealed only since his death, the verdict of the authorities has not been reversed. His approach to life was the approach not of the man of letters but of the man of action. Literary expression to him was never an end in itself, as it is to the true artist in

words, but merely a means to an end—a tool,
an instrument, a weapon. A phrase here or
there, a paragraph, one or two complete
essays suggest what he might have accomplished in literature if he had approached life
through the gate of contemplation rather than
through the gate of action. He did not care
enough for the making of literature ever to
write really great books. His countrymen,
perhaps, are fortunate that he did not. The
ability to make the steam rise between the
lines in such a way that the rhythm of the
words tells what words alone never can express, is as a rule incompatible with the ability greatly to act. The exception is Lincoln,
but passages which are literature are scarcely
less rare in Lincoln's writings than they are
in Roosevelt's. Too close attention to expression appears to create impediments and
inhibitions to the power of action and de-
cision. A man cannot at the same time run
a race and dwell on the physiology of bodily
propulsion, or fight a battle and linger over
the literary arrangement of the words of

command. As a rule absorption in expression exhausts the nervous energy to such an extent that the will or even the ability to act is enfeebled. Unconsciously, the golden phrase, the result of laborious intellectual or spiritual activity, appears to its creator as itself an act.

In Roosevelt's mind there was no room for such confusion. He knew and loved everything which was fine in literature, but he would have been a different man—and by no means necessarily a greater man—if he could ever have forced himself for long periods into the mood which is essential for the creation of literary masterpieces.

He was an immensely effective public speaker; no doubt the most effective of his time; but in what is commonly called oratory, in the building of impressive structures of argument (which might be sound or not), in emotional appeals swaying great crowds by the sheer force of eloquence, Bryan exceeded him and Bourke Cockran and Beveridge and Raymond Robins. He had none of the arts of the orator; he could handle a heckler with wit and despatch; but he made no attempt to play with his audiences or upon them. His sincerity and his zeal for righteousness, together with his mental and physical vigor and his ability to say what he had to say in words which were in common use, were the ingredients of his power in his direct contacts with great masses of people.

The apprehension with which opposing politicians regarded him suggests that as a politician he was a master. He had, in fact, superb qualifications for political leadership. His sympathy for the common man was whole-hearted and altogether unfeigned; he had real confidence in democratic institutions, and he knew better than any other man of his time the political value of courage. But it is worth noting that after he left the Presidency he was beaten in every political struggle in which he took part, except the last. As a politician he had one defect which was incorrigible—a grim insistence, in major matters, of following a line of conduct which he conceived to be right, regardless of personal considerations. It prevented him from becoming a candidate for the Presidency in 1908, when his re-election would have been assured; it cost him the Republican nomination in 1912, when a group of delegates offered to turn the vote in his favor if he would compromise on certain questions which to them were questions of detail but which to him happened to be questions of principle. The speech which he made at the height of the preconvention campaign of 1912, against the pleas of his advisers, advocating the recall of judicial decisions, was fatal in a nation whose political leaders are largely lawyers. He was as a rule almost uncanny in his understanding of popular sentiment, but he was less clear-sighted at times in estimating his own strength. He habitually underrated it, fatally in 1908, when he had the power to remake the Republican National Committee which wrecked the party's fortunes in 1912, and did not exercise it because he believed that the leaders would rebel against "dicta-

tion from the White House." The truth was
that he had the party in the hollow of his
hand.

I have suggested briefly what seem to me
to have been the limitations of Roosevelt's
achievement in a number of fields in which he
rendered distinguished service. His gifts as
a historian, a naturalist, a writer, an orator,
a politician had an important bearing on
what I conceive to have been his greatest
achievement; they were sources of incalcu-
lable power, or of relaxation invaluable to a
man of his consuming fire; they added enor-
mously to the richness of his personality.
But they do not themselves validate the
claim to surpassing service which, without
question, I, for one, would make for him.
In fact, they tend to obscure it. They provide too obvious an answer to the sceptic's
query; an answer too easy for the sceptic to
prove unsoundly based.

It is in a different field that Roosevelt's
true greatness, his supreme service, are to be
sought. In order that that greatness, that

service may stand out sharply and unmis-
takably, it is necessary to push aside the
minor gifts, the minor achievements, record-
ing them for what they were—the attractive
incidentals of a resplendent life and no more.
It is only by some such heroic sweeping aside
of non-essentials that it is possible to reveal
the fundamental significance of his life.

III

ROOSEVELT'S achievements as a statesman
were of two kinds: the obvious and tangible, which found expression in treaties and
statutes and, through such instruments, in
forest reserves, redeemed wildernesses, the
reform of the civil service, the movement of
fleets, the subjection of corporations and
labor organizations to the national will, peace
between warring nations, the building of a
great canal; and the intangible, which were
expressed in the changing attitude of a hundred million people toward politics and government, and the beginning of a new co-
hesion of antagonistic groups which the rapid

growth of the population and the material development of the country had created.

Roosevelt said more than once that he himself regarded the building of the Panama Canal and the voyage of the battle fleet around the world as the two outstanding achievements of his administration as President. His action in securing peace between Russia and Japan won for him the applause of the world, and the experts on the Far East who criticised his policy are only now beginning to apprehend the extent to which international politics on the continent of Europe were involved in a struggle which appeared to be localized in the Orient; and how effective Roosevelt's leadership was in preventing at that time the World War which came ten years later.* It is questionable, however, whether his struggle for the regulation of corporations, and his efforts in behalf of reclamation of waste areas and the conservation of natural resources, were not

* "Roosevelt and the Russo-Japanese War." By Tyler Dennett.

in the long run even more significant than
any of his diplomatic triumphs. The vision,
the energy, the courage, and the keen sense
of the national honor with which he administered his high office constituted in themselves a contribution of lasting value to
American tradition and gave the United
States a new prestige among the powers of
the world.

Roosevelt was unquestionably a successful
statesman; was he a great statesman? Was
he merely one who, using wisely the opportunities which his conspicuous place gave
him at home and abroad, solved brilliantly
certain immediate problems which he en-
countered; or was he of that small company
in the world's history who set in motion
forces which change the structure of society
and determine the attitude of generations yet
unborn to questions which involve the character of the government or even the existence
of the nation?

Justly to appraise Roosevelt's place in
world history, it is clear that here too there

must be a bold sweeping aside of incidentals
in order that the essentials may appear un-
obstructed. The triumph of his mediation in
the Russo-Japanese War; his success in ter-
minating the Venezuela imbroglio; even—
though it be heresy—the building of the
Canal and the voyage of the fleet, imposing
as these achievements were, appear, after the
passage of the years, rather the successes of a
vigorous, courageous, astute personality than
the products of spiritual vision and intellectual, moral, and spiritual travail. Roosevelt
himself on one occasion recognized them for
what they now appear, highly significant de-
tails of an infinitely larger enterprise. The
reverberations of these successes, moreover,
have either ceased already, or may cease.
The Panama Canal alone remains as the
material evidence of a prodigious personal
triumph. The Canal has, no doubt, affected
the material development of the West; it
has greatly facilitated the movement of
American fleets. The energetic manner in
which the problems were met which its con-

struction presented will continue to be a source of pride and inspiration to the American people. But the Canal would, sooner or later, have been built even if Roosevelt had not been President. It might, moreover, be destroyed or supplanted by a sea-level canal in Nicaragua, and the development of the American people would in all probability be unaffected. The Panama Canal is a monument to Roosevelt the executive, but it is a question whether with the essential element of Roosevelt's greatness as a statesman it is more than incidentally concerned.

The tangible achievements of Roosevelt stand clear and undisputed on the records of the thirty-eight years of his public life, which were cut exactly at the middle point by the coming of the new century. Treaties and legislative acts are easy to record; a date anchors them. The intangible, which are often the greater, triumphs elude altogether the spectacled eyes and the rough fingers of the annalist and frequently escape even the keener glance and the surer grasp of the historian. But it is on the intangible achievement that any permanent fame must always rest. The peasant in Russia, in the days of the Czar, nailed his picture of Abraham Lincoln on the wall not because Lincoln preserved a union of States which the peasant barely knew existed, but because out of Lincoln's words, backed by Lincoln's deeds, had gone forth across the seas the idea that no man is good enough to be another man's master; and the face that he honored was the symbol of that truth. In the case of all truly great men the tangible and the intangible achievements are intertwined, the intangible again and again finding expression in the tangible, and the tangible providing a point of leverage for other, deeper, scarcely discernible dynamic impulsions.

In Roosevelt the qualities of moral leadership and practical executive force were combined in a degree scarcely paralleled in history. His words were constantly becoming actions either through others, whom he influenced, or in obedience to his own will; and his actions were often, by design, agencies for the propagation of ideas. He had the rare and invaluable gift of dramatizing every question which he touched. Abstract ideas with him took body and blood, and walked familiarly, as it were, over the threshold of the simplest dwelling.

IV

ROOSEVELT was the first American President to recognize fully the real source of whatever power he possessed. During his Presidency, as in other periods of his career that preceded or followed it, when the politicians blocked his way, he thrust the politicians aside and laid his case before the people. He appealed to them for support and they gave it, and with it they gave a measure of affection which few leaders of men have been able to evoke. Possibly those who gave most knew least why they gave it. They liked his force, his fearlessness, his large heart, his embracing understanding, his human sympathy, his evident and unquestionable delight in the fellowship and the confidence of the common man, his exuberance, his indiscretion, his lack of "side," of Presidential pomposity. But those qualities endeared him to them less, perhaps, than the fact that, in a way which they could not themselves explain, he made them desire to be better men. The words he spoke were simple words which they could all understand; the matters he talked about were the matters which were closest to their own hearts. He spoke of elemental things, of home and wife and children, of daily labor for daily bread, of duty and service and sacrifice, first in the little world within their own four walls, then in the world just outside, and then in the world beyond that. He made them see that the great service was only the small service writ large, and that the small service honestly and effectively done linked them with him and with all others who were thus giving service in great fields or small.

With large strokes he painted the needs of the nation before their eyes, describing the

huge unknown thing in terms of the simple
familiar thing which they knew. He reduced
complicated economic problems which were
over their heads to simple questions of right
and wrong which they understood. He reinterpreted American institutions to them.
Their own forebodings and aspirations became intelligible to them through his words.
He crystallized their cloudy musings.
"Through you we have been reborn in character and mind," was the tribute which an
associate paid him at that last meeting of
the Tennis Cabinet the day before Roosevelt left the Presidency, when hardened
"two-gun men" broke down. He gave utterance to the best that was in their own
hearts, and in responding to him they were
conscious that they were responding to im-
pulses which they had themselves felt and
had been unable to express. He gave vital-
ity to the best aspirations of their own na-
tures and showed them how those aspirations might find expression. He belted their
consciences to the machinery of government.

Under his spell men rediscovered their country and took pride in her and came to feel a personal responsibility for her welfare and honor. He made them desire not safety but the doing of difficult things. He made them want to do their duty; he made them ashamed not to want to do their duty. He led them to the hill of vision and made them dream dreams; and, when it came to fighting for the promised land, it was always he who was in the forefront of the hottest battle.

The people he led and served felt instinctively that he was different from other great men they had known or read about; at bottom an average man; "an ordinary man," as he said of himself on one occasion, disclaiming all pretensions to genius, "with ordinary qualities extraordinarily developed." That powers and triumphs such as his should come to one so like themselves and their neighbors was to them a new reason for faith in the democratic idea.

It would be difficult to exaggerate the significance of Roosevelt's part in that great

movement which seeks to lift the standard of
human government and to enlarge and purify
the individual, by giving him the rights which
make men self-respecting and the responsi-
bilities which develop character. It was the
supreme achievement of Washington, himself an aristocrat, in his time, to establish a
government on the theory of equality of opportunity and responsibility. Lincoln, a
man of the people, demonstrated, in his
cycle, that the theory was sound and that
character, honor, integrity, intellect, administrative power, vision, transcendent genius
may as likely be found in cabins, half-open to
the storm, as in stately houses and in uni-
versities. Roosevelt, in his turn, with Washington and Lincoln as his greatest heroes,
made the sense of brotherhood, on which
democracy is ultimately based, for splendid
moments a reality.

It was not only that he felt like a brother
to others. There are many who, in exalted
moments, experience that emotion. The significant thing is that the others felt like

brothers to him. People who had never seen
him, who had never come within range of
his galvanizing personality or of the sound of
his voice, regarded him as somehow closer
and dearer to them than blood brothers oft-
en are. When he died men wept who had
shed no tears at the death of a father or a
brother. It was not that, as Americans, they
mourned the loss of a leader whom they
knew their country most bitterly needed.
They wept because they had lost what in
the old West used to be known as a "pard-
ner," the bunkmate, the man to whom in
spirit at least they could pour out their
troubles and their shy, tenuous aspirations,
knowing that he would understand. The
world was suddenly appallingly empty, like a
house from which the companion of a lifetime has been taken.

There has been no other leader, perhaps,
in American life who has borne that re-
lationship to countless thousands of the
American people. "When you get among the
rough, poor, honest, hard-working people,"

wrote his old friend, Bill Sewall, "they are almost all, both men and women, believers in Roosevelt." There were cultivated men and women, of wealth and social standing, who believed in him as passionately as any, but it was among the poor, among the struggling, that he was best beloved.

Many men have talked of brotherhood in the abstract, but their words never came to life. Roosevelt talked about it little if at all, but inevitably and without pretense he lived it, and Tom and Dick and Harry and Susan and Mary and Jane—brakeman and farmer and millionaire, school-teacher and working girl and prairie mother—felt it instinctively and overwhelmingly, and gave him the keys to the city.

V

ROOSEVELT was a supreme leader of the people; to what high goal did he direct their steps?

As a young man his first public act was a charge against a venal judge, and all his life long he fought against corruption in municipal, State, and national government. From his earliest days in the political arena the Macedonian cry resounds and re-echoes through his life: "Come over and help us!" He stirred powerfully the imaginations of young men and enlisted their energies in the service of honest and intelligent government. They listened to him when he was an Assemblyman, they flocked to him when he was Civil Service Commissioner and Police Commissioner; they acclaimed him as their leader when he was Governor and President. He insisted, day in, day out, that rights entailed duties, and that political duties were not limited to the occasional casting of a vote. He showed what needed to be done; he showed the practical way of meeting the need; he appealed to reason and to patriotism, to manhood and to the heritage of heroic traditions. Day after day, touring the country as Governor, as President, or as a private citizen, he reiterated the same essential message: we need honesty, but honesty is useless if it is merely negative; we need, in addition, courage, but both honesty and courage are useless "if a man is a natural-born fool"; we need three things: honesty, courage, and common sense.

"Thou shalt not steal!" he declared alike to the rich man who utilized "inside information" to plunder innocent stockholders, and to the poor man who wanted to wipe out his debts with "easy money." *"Thou shalt not lie!"* he thundered alike to the mendacious journalist and to the politician who made promises which he knew he could not or would not carry out. "The liar and the thief," he maintained, "stand on the same level of evil eminence." Scarcely beneath them he placed that part of the public which, by its indolence or indifference, permitted liar and thief to get away with the loot.

He preached respect for the things of the body, not because they had value of and by themselves but because the loftiest teachings are ineffective if the teacher "exists at all only because his wife takes in washing." He urged that every man "carry his own weight," provide for and protect those that are dependent on him, meet first of all the common, obvious needs; asking that the neighbor who falls should be lifted but declaring that the neighbor who insists on being carried is not worth the carrying. He pleaded for the two sets of qualities—for tenderness and strength, pointing out again and again, and not without humor, the ineffectiveness of sweetness unsupported by power, and the peril of strength uncontrolled by such "gentilnesse," as Chaucer exalted in his model knight. To exact justice was to him no less essential than to give justice. In personal as in national life he insisted that a policy of milk and water was scarcely less reprehensible than a policy of blood and iron. In driving home his doctrine that softness of head was no more admirable a quality than hardness of heart, he enjoyed quoting Artemus Ward's famous dictum: "It is easier to be a simple dove than a wise serpent."

Wherever he went he preached the glory of endeavor.

He pleaded for the quality of daring in national as well as in personal life, for the large vision, the lofty conception, the "heroic mood." Against the sordid appeal of *Safety First*, he preached the stern doctrine of duty and service and sacrifice.

"In peace and war we must spend and be spent, in the endless battle for right against wrong," he wrote during the Great War. "Deeds, not words, alone can save us. . . . To my fellow Americans I preach the sword of the Lord and of Gideon. . . . Let us pay with our bodies for our souls' desire!"

He preached always realizable ideals—ideals a little beyond the reach, but not so far beyond that the intrepid and aspiring heart might not conceivably attain them; ideals that concerned themselves not with things afar but with things close at hand, ideals which were not stars so much as stepping-stones. With his practical mind, believing in the capacity of mankind to pro-

gress, yet conscious always of mankind's in-
nate conservatism and reluctance to relin-
quish its prejudices and its traditional approach to the fundamental problems of
existence, and aware, moreover, of the con-
vulsions it had always cost "each painful
inch to gain," he preached the progress not
of leaps and bounds, not of sudden soarings
into the alien atmosphere of sidereal space,
but the less dramatic, slower, surer progress
of stride by human stride.

Now and then, in a crisis, a great people,
led by a great man, might at white heat strike
some mighty blow for the right or, filled
with a divine impulsion, take a long stride in
advance along the path of justice and orderly
liberty; but normally, he declared, men must
be content to do the little things which, in
the aggregate, make for the advancement of
those principles of righteousness which under-
lie true civilization. Man's success in accom-
plishing anything, he pointed out again and
again, depends largely upon his not trying to
accomplish everything. He warned against

patent cure-alls for every ill of the body politic. "A medicine that is recommended to cure both asthma and a broken leg," he would say, "is not good for either."

The philosophy which he unfolded was simple, coherent, and complete; a pyramid, whose broad base were the elemental virtues and whose apex was the communion of nations. All his moral, social, political, and economic ideas group themselves about five fundamental conceptions, bound together into one compact and aspiring whole, in which the elemental virtues stand as the basis of good citizenship; good citizenship the basis of just government; just government the basis of national unity; national unity the basis of national strength; national strength the basis of international peace.

He did not, it is worth repeating, speak much of the brotherhood of man—such vague and resounding conceptions appeared to him to belong not to the field of political discussion at all but to the field of metaphysics, for which he had no sympathy—but he urged day after day a greater sense of responsibility of each man for his neighbor and a "square deal" for all men.

"All of us in our present civilization," he said in effect again and again, "are dependent upon one another to a degree never before known in the history of mankind, and in the long run we are going to go up or go down together. For a moment some man may rise by trampling on his fellows; for a moment, and much more commonly, some men may think they will rise or gratify their envy and hatred by pulling down others. But any such movement upward is probably illusory, and is certainly short-lived. Any permanent movement upward must come in such a shape that all of us feel the lift a little, and if there is a tendency downward all of us will feel that tendency too. We must, if we are to raise ourselves, realize that each of us in the long run can with certainty be raised only if the conditions are such that all of us are somewhat raised."

During the Progressive campaign he

summed up this doctrine in one simple, immortal sentence: "This country will not be a really good place for any of us to live in if it is not a reasonably good place for all of us to live in."

In this restatement of the old American motto, "United we stand, divided we fall," beats the heart of Roosevelt's message to his time and to the generations to be.

VI

ROOSEVELT had many gifts, many interests, varied and picturesque, many aims which he pursued with all the perseverance of his indomitable mind, many enthusiasms; and with them he had one great passion.

It is not hard to guess where and when the first faint flicker of that passion was kindled. He woke to consciousness as a reasoning being just at the opening of what proved the most terrible civil war in world history. His father was of the North, his mother of the South; both were ardent and tenacious partisans; but with a singular loftiness of soul they kept their relations to each other and to the home free from bitterness. In such an atmosphere the hatred which a patriot conceives too easily for the enemies of his country and of what he believes to be the right could not thrive; in such a household there would be little rancor, but much pity. The father's devotion to the Union communicated itself to his son; from him the son, no doubt, acquired his loathing for the "copperhead," which showed itself at intervals throughout his life and flamed up furiously in his last years—the soul which is neither hot nor cold, being too meticulous, too finely balanced, too conscious of the rights of the wrong side and the wrongs of the right side to support a cause whole-heartedly; and too cowardly openly to oppose it.

What impressions of the madness and the pitifulness of disunion must have been burned into the mind and spirit of the ardent young American! Disunion among the States, disunion within the States! It is not strange that in such a boy, at such a time, should have been born a passion for national unity.

That passion burned in Roosevelt from his youth to the day of his death. It found expression in his efforts to complete the healing of the breach between North and South, and his endeavor to make East and West understand one another; it flamed out fiercely in his denunciations of religious intolerance. It never burned more brightly than in his fight against division in the American people on lines of race or land of origin; or woke in his mind a deeper, surer vision than in his long and effective struggle against the menace of social, economic, and industrial cleavage.

Throughout his life Roosevelt fought many battles, in many high causes, but at bottom it was one cause, one supreme cause which he was always serving, the solidarity of the American people. The nation which Washington founded and Lincoln preserved, Roosevelt consolidated.

VII

AMONG the great consequences of a little war, Roosevelt was always convinced that one of the greatest was the spiritual reunion of the North and South which the common effort in behalf of Cuba inaugurated. Speaking in every part of the country during the years that followed the war, he lost no opportunity to emphasize with what complete fraternity the sons of men who had worn the blue had striven at the side of the sons of men who had served the gray, under commanders who had begun their careers as soldiers, some in the army of Grant, some in the army of Lee. Side by side with Young and Chaffee and Lawton, he pointed out, Wheeler and Fitzhugh Lee had served; and in his own regiment the sons of ex-Confederates had been as many as the sons of those who had fought in the Union armies. Those "children of the dragon's blood" had known no cleavage, standing shoulder to shoulder, "knit together by the closest of ties, and acknowledging with respect to one another only that generous jealousy each to try to be first to do all that in him lay for the honor and the interest of the flag that covered the reunited country."

He took great pride in the heroism of his own Southern kin, and with his unfailing sense of the dramatic utilized at every opportunity the fact that he was himself half of the North and half of the South in endeavoring to complete the healing of the breach between the sections. Wherever he went in the South, he emphasized this sense of personal kinship, glorying in the valor of the past and the renewed energy and enterprise of the present. He took a personal pride in the material prosperity of the new South, in the growth of its cities, the growth of its educational facilities. It was in order, on the one hand, to show his personal interest and the interest of the national government, and, on the other, to bring vividly before the imagination of the North the trials under which a Southern city was suffering, that, during the yellow-fever epidemic in New Orleans, at the risk of his life, he visited the stricken community.

As Civil Service Commissioner he went out of his way to bring hundreds of young Southerners—Democrats in the main—into the government service under a Republican administration. Several of his personal aides as President were Southerners. He made a Tennessean, General Luke Wright, Governor of the Philippines and later Secretary of War. He rejoiced in the triumph of the spirit of unity over the spirit of dissension, which made such appointments possible.

In the South it was always the consciousness of a reunited country that was in the forefront of his mind. Again and again this consciousness found eloquent expression.

"Oh, my fellow countrymen," he said a dozen times, "think what a blessed thing it is that now every man in this land can feel the same pride in the valor and devotion of those who fought for one side and of those who fought for the other!"

At the conclusion of his address during the epidemic in New Orleans, it was to the glory of reunion that he gave his final words:

"Oh, my fellow countrymen, think what a fortune is ours, that we belong to this nation, which, having fought one of the mightiest wars of all times, is now reunited forever, in an indissoluble union, under one flag; so that we claim as ours the heritage of honor and glory left by every man who, on whichever side he stood, when the days came which tried men's souls, did all that in him lay—did his whole duty—according to the light that was given him to see that duty."

The one remaining vestige of Southern sectionalism, the political solidarity of the South, greatly occupied his mind. It has been said that one of the reasons he organized the Progressive party was his hope that a new party, based on issues which were equally vital to all the States of the Union, might break the solid South, revitalize its political life, and bring the separate States which composed it into closer sympathy with the States of the North and West. Against the wishes of his campaign managers, who believed that he could serve the Progressive cause more effectively in parts of the country where the old party lines were less rigidly fixed, he toured the South in 1912. He scarcely expected to win any of the Southern States, but he hoped that his effort might prepare the ground for another's reaping. In the South Atlantic and Gulf States as a whole he recognized that there was no real Republican party, nor any indication that in these States the Republican party could ever be built up. He hoped that the Progressive party would supply this deficiency, not only for the sake of these States themselves but for the sake of the whole Union. It seemed to him an unhealthy and an unnatural thing for the Southern States and for the nation (as well as for the Democratic party itself) that there should, in effect, be no opposition party and no opportunity for the men who were in principle opposed to the Democratic party to give expression to their principles in such a manner as would be possible if they dwelt in other sections of the Union where there was a normal division on party lines.

The sense of unity which he sought to bring about between the various sections of the country he himself felt in every fibre of his being. "I am not sectional," he said to Captain Archie Butt,* his military aide. "I haven't got a sectional bone in my body. I imbibed the traditions and folk-lore of the South from my mother; my earliest training and principles were Southern; I sought the West of my own accord, and my manhood has largely been fought out in the North."

He decried attempts in literature as in politics to develop an "unwholesome, parochial spirit, that over-exaltation of the little community at the expense of the great nation which produces what has been described as the patriotism of the village, the patriotism of the belfry." He had no pa-

* "The Letters of Archie Butt." Doubleday, Page & Company.

tience with talk of a Northern literature or a
Southern literature, an Eastern or a Western
school of art or science. Joel Chandler Harris
and Mark Twain, he pointed out, were alike
the pride of all Americans.

More keenly, perhaps, than any other
American statesman he felt a sense of kinship with every portion of the American people. He knew the whole country as few public men have known it. Where he had not
hunted or driven cattle, he had worked on
his historical studies, or made inspections as
Civil Service Commissioner, or addressed
great crowds during political campaigns, or
visited with all manner of men on Presidential "swings around the circle." He had
travelled from the Atlantic to the Pacific,
from the Great Lakes to the Gulf, he had
spoken at country fairs, to colleges, to com-
mercial and business organizations, to asso-
ciations of professional men, to labor organizations, to men of every creed and parentage.
Wherever he went he preached his doctrine of
the interdependence of the individual of

every section and race and religion on every
other individual; and it stirred him that
everywhere he experienced "the essential
oneness, the essential unity," of the American
people.

He emphasized this unity not only in the
South. He was aware that the West was
growing away from the East, gradually but
no less certainly than in the early years of
the preceding century the South had grown
away from the North. The Populist movement, culminating in the Presidential campaign of 1896, had shown him how easily,
under the spur of want and prejudice, a new
cleavage by sections might be created.
Speaking in San Francisco in 1903, he said:

"I have come from the Atlantic across this
continent to the Pacific. I have greeted many
audiences. I see a little diversity, but, oh,
my countrymen, what strikes me most and
pleases me most is the fundamental unity, is
the fact that wherever I go I speak to an
audience of Americans, be they East or be
they West. And I make the same appeal

with the same confidence, here beside the
Golden Gate, that I would make by the
Great Lakes or in the upper Mississippi
Valley or on the Atlantic Ocean. This is a
government of free men, who have achieved
liberty under the law, who have, by force of
arms as well as by legislation, established
once for all, as the fundamental principle of
our government, that there shall not in this
country be license; that there shall not be in
this country liberty to oppress without the
law; that liberty and freedom shall come under and in pursuance of the law, of the law
that is no respecter of persons, under a government that is a government neither for the
rich man as such nor for the poor man as
such, but for every man, rich or poor, if he is
a decent man and does his duty to the state."

Apart from his direct appeal for national
unity against sectional isolation, his own
continual preaching, in every corner of the
country, of the American conception of liberty common to all his hearers was a powerful force in the consolidation of the nation.

A force, even more powerful, was his own
personality. When he said of himself that he
was not sectional, he gave expression to a
truth which his fellow citizens of every section of the country recognized. The North
and East naturally claimed him because of
his birth; the South, which periodically rose
in indignation against him, could not deny a
fondness for him and an ineradicable pride in
him as a son of Georgia. The West, however,
claimed him as peculiarly her own. She
might have said, with truth, that in her he
had found his second birth. He was, in a
very vital sense, a mediator between the East
and West; through him they came to understand each other as they had never understood each other before. It is no exaggera-
tion to say that in the first decade of the
century his personality was the most vital
factor in the abatement of the rising feeling
of the " insurgent " West against the economic
and political dominance of the East.

PROPHET OF UNITY

VIII

HE fought against sectionalism no more
vigorously or more ardently than he fought
against that more insidious breeder of dissension and creator of cleavage, religious intolerance. He was himself a Protestant, but
two of his closest advisers and most treasured
friends were Catholics, Charles J. Bonaparte
and Father Curran. The story how, in his
Police Commissioner days, he protected an
apprehensive anti-Semite lecturer with a
squad of police carefully selected for their
obviously Semitic origin, is familiar. He de-
tested anti-Semitism as heartily as he de-
tested the bigotry of the fanatical adherents
and opponents of Roman Catholicism. He
was the first and he has remained the only
American President to appoint a Jew to his
Cabinet. He appointed Oscar Straus for his
statesmanship, proved previously and there-
after, but he admitted privately that it rejoiced his soul that his new secretary happened to be a Jew, as he was thus enabled to

dramatize to the American people his own insistence that no questions of race or creed should bar any loyal citizen from the highest places in the gift of the people.

It was not political expediency but a principle which he regarded as fundamental that underlay his efforts to break down the barriers of religious prejudice.

"We are Americans," he said at the banquet of the Sons of the American Revolution in Washington in 1902, "and that means that we treat Americanism primarily as a matter of spirit and purpose, and in the broadest sense we regard every man as a good American, whatever his creed, whatever his birthplace, if he is true to the ideals of this Republic."

Once, toward the end of his administration, his passionate aversion to anything resembling religious cleavage, burst from him in hot anger. It was immediately after the election of Mr. Taft. Numerous letters had come to him during the course of the campaign inquiring concerning the candidate's religious views. It was rumored that he was a Unitarian (an "infidel" from the standpoint of the writers) and that his wife and his brother were Roman Catholics.

"While it is claimed universally that religion should not enter politics," wrote one perturbed spirit from Ohio, "yet there is no denying that it does, and the mass of the voters that are not Catholics will not support a man for any office, especially for President of the United States, who is a Roman Catholic. . . . On the other hand, if he is an infidel, that would be sure to mean defeat."

In order that the issue might not be obscured in the excitement of the campaign and because he regarded it "as an outrage even to agitate such a question as a man's religious conviction, with the purpose of influencing a political election," he waited until the campaign was over to send his reply to the slander which he declared his correspondent had uttered against all Americans.

"To discriminate against a thoroughly upright citizen because he belongs to some particular church," he wrote, "or because, like Abraham Lincoln, he has not avowed his allegiance to any church, is an outrage against that liberty of conscience which is one of the foundations of American life. You are entitled to know whether a man seeking your suffrages is a man of clean and upright life, honorable in all of his dealings with his fellows, and fit by qualification and purpose to do well in the great office for which he is a candidate; but you are not entitled to know matters which lie purely between himself and his Maker. If it is proper or legitimate to oppose a man for being a Unitarian, as was John Quincy Adams, for instance, as is the Rev. Edward Everett Hale, at the present moment Chaplain of the Senate, and an American of whose life all good Americans are proud—then it would be equally proper to support or oppose a man because of his views on justification by faith, or the methods of administering the sacrament, or the gospel of salvation by works. If you once enter on such a career there is absolutely no limit at which you can legitimately stop.

"So much for your objections to Mr. Taft because he is a Unitarian. Now, for your objections to him because you think his wife and brother to be Roman Catholics. As it happens, they are not; but if they were, or if he were a Roman Catholic himself, it ought not to affect in the slightest degree any man's supporting him for the position of President. You say that 'the mass of the voters that are not Catholics will not support a man for any office, especially for President of the United States, who is a Roman Catholic.' I believe that when you say this you foully slander your fellow countrymen. I do not for one moment believe that the mass of our fellow citizens, or that any considerable number of our fellow citizens, can be influenced by such narrow bigotry as to refuse to vote for any thoroughly upright and fit man because he happens to have a particular religious creed. Such a consideration should never be treated as a reason for either supporting or opposing a candidate for a political office. . . .

"I believe that this Republic will endure for many centuries. If so there will doubtless

be among its Presidents Protestants and
Catholics, and, very probably at some time,
Jews. I have consistently tried while President to act in relation to my fellow Americans
of Catholic faith as I hope that any future
President who happens to be a Catholic will
act toward his fellow Americans of Protestant faith. Had I followed any other course
I should have felt that I was unfit to represent the American people.

"In my Cabinet at the present moment
there sit side by side Catholic and Protestant, Christian and Jew, each man chosen
because in my belief he is peculiarly fit to
exercise on behalf of all our people the duties
of the office to which I have appointed him.
In no case does the man's religious belief in
any way influence his discharge of his duties,
save as it makes him more eager to act
justly and uprightly in his relations to all
men. The same principles that have obtained
in appointing the members of my Cabinet,
the highest officials under me, the officials to
whom is intrusted the work of carrying out

all the important policies of my administration, are the principles upon which all good Americans should act in choosing, whether by election or appointment, the men to fill any office from the highest to the lowest in the land."

Again and again he insisted that it was essential that every citizen should have the right to hold and to express religious views which best met "his own soul needs." Any political movement directed against any body of Americans because of their religious creed he regarded as the greatest possible offense against American principles and American institutions. Political movements directed against certain individuals because of their religious belief had never accomplished anything but harm; and such movements, he insisted, directly contravened the spirit of the Constitution itself. The founders of the Republic had believed that it was essential to the existence of the nation that there should be no union of church and state; and such union, he pointed out, was partially accomplished wherever a given creed was aided by the States, or when any public servant was elected or defeated because of his creed. The Constitution explicitly forbids any religious test as a qualification for holding office. To impose such a test by popular vote, he declared, was as bad as to impose it by law. To vote either for or against a man because of his creed was to impose upon him a religious test, and was a clear violation of the spirit of the Constitution.

He pointed out, moreover, that such movements never achieved the end they nominally had in view, actually doing nothing whatsoever except to increase among the men of the various churches the spirit of sectarian intolerance, "which is base and unlovely in any civilization, but which is utterly revolting among free people that profess the principles we profess." No such movement, he declared, could ever permanently succeed in this country. All that it might do would be for a decade or more to increase the spirit of theological animosity both among the people to whom it appealed and among the people whom it assailed. The result in the end, as a rule, was merely to place unworthy men in office. "For there is nothing that a man of loose principles and of evil practices in public life so desires as the chance to distract attention from his own shortcomings and misdeeds by exciting and inflaming theological and sectarian prejudice."

He insisted that the surest way to bring failure on any movement to better political conditions was to inject religious proscription into it. In citing on one occasion the help he, as a Republican and a Protestant, born in America, had received as Police Commissioner from a certain Democrat, a Catholic, born in Ireland, Roosevelt asked: "Can you imagine anything at the same time more absurd and more criminal than that we American citizens should carry into the kind of contest which we have waged differences of creed? Can you imagine a surer way to compass the defeat of a movement for good than by allowing it to be complicated by any question of creed?"

He opposed parochial schools; but, he pointed out, "when we say that we want our schools to be non-sectarian we must mean what we say." When he was Civil Service Commissioner it was characteristic of him that he should go out of his way to support a ticket for school trustees in Boston, composed of Catholics and Protestants, because the opposing ticket, no stronger than the other from an educational standpoint, was composed exclusively of Protestants. "I esteem myself the stanchest friend of the public-school system for so doing," he declared, "and I esteem our opponents the worst foes of the public-school system for the course that they took."

"We must recognize," he maintained, "that it is a cardinal sin against Democracy to support a man for public office because he belongs to a given creed or to oppose him because he belongs to a given creed. It is just as evil to draw the line between class and

class, as between occupation and occupation
in political life. No man who tries to draw
either line is a good American. True Americanism demands that we judge each man on
his conduct, that we so judge him in private
life and that we so judge him in public life.
The line of cleavage drawn on principle and
conduct in public affairs is never in any
healthy community identical with the line of
cleavage between creed and creed or between
class and class."

IX

ROOSEVELT fought for national solidarity
with what was almost his dying breath. A
few hours before in the solitude and silence
of night, without warning, the valiant heart
ceased to beat, his final message, read in his
absence, rang through a huge assembly in
New York.

"There must be no sagging back in the
fight for Americanism merely because the
war is over. Any man who says he is an
American, and something else also, isn't an

American at all. We have room for but one
flag, the American flag. . . . We have room
for but one language here, and that is the
English language . . . and we have room
for but one soul loyalty, and that is loyalty
to the American people."

In this message culminated and ended a
struggle for the spiritual unity of "the children of the crucible" on which Roosevelt had
been engaged during the whole of his public
career.

In the only public address which he delivered in the West during the years of his
activity as a ranchman, he drove home almost in the same words that he used again
and again during the years of the Great War
the oneness of the American people, regardless of race or creed.

"All American citizens," he said at Dickin-
son, Dakota, in 1886, "whether born here or
elsewhere, whether of one creed or another,
stand on the same footing. We welcome every
honest immigrant no matter from what country he comes, provided only that he leaves

off his former nationality, and remains neither Celt nor Saxon, neither Frenchman nor German, but becomes an American, desirous of fulfilling in good faith the duties of American citizenship."

Year in, year out, he preached that doctrine with characteristic ardor. Where immigrants, or the sons of immigrants, did not heartily and in good faith throw in their lot with the American people but clung to the speech, the customs, the ways of life, and the habits of thought of the Old World which they had left, remaining alien, unassimilated elements, he insisted that they were obstructions to the current of the national life and a menace to American institutions. It was to him clearly in the immigrant's own interest as speedily as possible to adapt himself to American customs and to adjust his mind to American ideas of government and society; it was unquestionably in the nation's interest. Americans had a right and more than a right, a duty, to demand that the alien accept American institutions and American ideals. He must slough off old allegiances, leave behind him old religious race and national antipathies, and must not be permitted to confuse the issues with which the American people were struggling by introducing among them Old World quarrels and prejudices. If America were to become and to remain in the truest sense a nation, her political and social questions, he insisted, must be settled on their own merits, and not complicated by quarrels between England and Ireland, or France and Germany, with which Americans have nothing to do. To him it was an outrage that an American political campaign should ever be fought with reference to questions of European politics. The immigrant, moreover, must learn to take pride in the things in which all Americans can take pride. He must revere only one flag; not only must it come first, but no other flag must ever come second. "Where two flags are hoisted on the same staff," he would say, "it is always the American flag which hangs below." Above all, "the immigrant must

learn to talk and think and be United States."
There must be no looking back to the various
Old World countries, no "Lot's-wife atti-
tude."

In ringing words he pointed out the danger of permitting the alien newcomers to live
together in communities governed not by
American habits of thought and American
traditions of government, but by German or
Irish or Polish or Hungarian traditions. The
one certain way of bringing the nation to
ruin, he declared, of preventing all possibility of its continuing to be a nation at all, was
to permit it to become "a tangle of squab-
bling nationalities," an intricate knot of
German-Americans, Irish-Americans, Eng-
lish-Americans, French-Americans, Scandi-
navian-Americans, or Italian-Americans, each
preserving its own nationality, each at heart
feeling more sympathy with Europeans of
that nationality than with the other citizens
of the Republic.

"We Americans are the children of the
crucible," he said in effect again and again

during the years of the Great War. "The crucible does not do its work unless it turns out those cast into it in one national mould; and that must be the mould established by Washington and his fellows when they made us a nation."

He made his appeal not only for undivided and undiluted loyalty, but for a deeper thing —unhesitating and unswerving acceptance of the fundamental principles of American institutions. It was with a glowing vision before his eyes that he pleaded for this profounder allegiance not of the mind only but of the heart and of the spirit.

"This is a new nation," he declared, "based on a mighty continent, of boundless possibilities. No other nation in the world has such resources. No other nation has ever been so favored. If we dare to rise level to the opportunities offered us, our destiny will be vast beyond the power of imagination. We must master this destiny, and make it our own; and we can thus make it our own only if we, as a vigorous and separate nation, develop a great and wonderful nationality, distinctively different from any other nationality, of either the present or the past. For such a nation all of us can well afford to give up all other allegiances, and high of heart, to stand, a mighty and united people, facing a future of glorious promise.

"This nation was founded because the Americans of 1776, although predominantly English by blood, fought their own kinsmen to establish their liberty and to make this nation the hope of the world. Again, over a century ago, our forefathers once more fought England; and the men in this country who were of English blood stood with absolute loyalty by America and against England. It is not merely our right but our duty to insist on exactly the same full-hearted loyalty by all Americans of other descent, whenever we are at war with the countries from which their ancestors came."

As always, he dramatized his argument. He spoke of American heroes—of Washington and Lincoln, of English extraction; of

Sullivan and Sheridan, of Irish extraction; of Schuyler and Van Buren, of Dutch extraction; of Muhlenberg and Herkimer and Sigel and Custer, of German extraction; of Marion and Beauregard, of French extraction. He spoke of his own Cabinet as President, in which a descendant of one of Blücher's colonels sat next to a grandnephew of Napoleon Bonaparte; of his work as Police Commissioner, in which some of his strongest allies had been Americans of Danish or German or Irish parentage; of the Rough Riders, in which every European strain had been represented; of the Division he had hoped to raise for the war against Germany, in which four colonels, a brigadier or two, a quartermaster-general and countless lesser officers were to have been men of German parentage or descent. As for himself, "it would take seven hyphens," he would say, "if any one tried to hyphenate me."

"Americanism is a question of spirit, conviction, and purpose, not of creed or birthplace. . . . That man is the best American who has in him the American spirit, the American soul."

In his struggle against the menace of cleavage on lines of race, he addressed his adjurations as much to the native American as to the newcomer.

"There are two demands upon the spirit of Americanism, of nationalism," he insisted. "Each must be met. Each is essential. Each is vital, if we are to be a great and proud nation.

"The first is that we shall tolerate no kind of divided allegiance in this country. There is no room for the hyphen in our citizenship. There is no place for a fifty-fifty Americanism in the United States. He who is not with us, absolutely and without reserve of any kind, is against us. This war has shown us in vivid and startling fashion the danger of allowing our people to separate along lines of racial origin and linguistic cleavage. We shall be guilty of criminal folly if we fail to insist on the complete and thoroughgoing unification of our people.

"This is one of the demands to be made in the name of the spirit of American nationalism. The other is equally important: We must treat every good American of German or of any other origin, without regard to his creed, as on a full and exact equality with every other good American, and set our faces like flint against the creatures who seek to discriminate against such an American, or to hold against him the birthplace of himself or his parents."

Those words, written in 1918, defined the principle on which he himself acted throughout his public career. In 1895, speaking in behalf of Americanism in municipal politics, he drove that principle home with sledge-hammer strokes. "The one being abhorrent to the powers above the earth and under them is the hyphenated American," he declared, "the 'German-American,' the 'Irish-American,' or the 'native-American.' Be Americans, pure and simple! If you don't act on the theory that every man who in good faith assumes the duties and responsi-

bilities of an American citizen in a spirit of
true Americanism is an American, and is to
be treated as such, if you do not act in that
spirit, you are yourselves unfit to take part
in managing our government."

Any discrimination against aliens, he insisted, was a wrong, because it tended to put
the immigrant at a disadvantage and to
cause him to feel bitterness and resentment
during the very years when he should be pre-
paring himself for American citizenship. If
an immigrant were not fit to become a citizen, he should not be allowed to enter the
country; if he were fit, he should be given
every right to earn his own livelihood and to
better himself that any man could have.
The nation, he knew, could not afford and,
he insisted, must not permit the use of hundreds of thousands of immigrants merely as
industrial assets "while they remain social
outcasts and menaces," any more than a half
century before the nation could afford to
keep the black man merely as an industrial
asset and not as a human being. There must

be a fusion of all the white races which come to America's shores, a fusion of interests, of aspirations; finally, of blood; the creation of a new American type, and loyalty to that type. Such loyalty, he declared, could not be invoked unless the stranger within the gates recognized that justice was being done him and that from him was exacted rightfully therefor the performance of corresponding duties.

"We must resolutely refuse to permit our great nation, our great America, to be split into a score of little replicas of European nationalities, and to become a Balkan penin-sula on a larger scale. We are a nation and not a hodgepodge of foreign nationalities. We are a people, and not a polyglot boarding-house. We must insist on a unified national-ity, with one flag, one language, one set of national ideals."

With a devotion which rose above all con-sideration of his own political fortunes and of bodily affliction, and with a fervor scarcely excelled by the fervor with which Washington strove for the nation's existence and Lincoln struggled for the nation's preservation, Roosevelt fought for the nation's unity. Day after day, month after month, throughout the Great War, in magazine articles and newspaper editorials, and in speeches delivered with unfaltering courage and vehemence in the very communities where the gospel that he preached was least welcome, he drove that gospel home. With the fiery intensity of a seer and a prophet, he trumpeted the glory of the American conception of a people united not by bonds of blood and common origin but by the spiritual tie of common devotion to the ideal of political freedom.

In the struggle, which is not ended, which may perhaps have only barely begun, the struggle for national unity against racial cleavage, Roosevelt rendered a service whose reverberations will make themselves felt as long as American institutions endure. He stated a principle which no one before him had stated so compellingly; he waged a battle whose effects no man can estimate, and

no heedless generation can wipe out. This or
that racial group may and no doubt will
yet fight in the open or under cover for racial
solidarity and political power, but, because
Roosevelt lived, it will be an up-hill fight,
with the odds against the enemy.

X

Roosevelt's last prodigious struggle for
unity was perhaps his most dramatic, for
its protagonist was a man stricken with ill-
ness and grief and set against a background
of a world in flames. But, far-reaching as it
was, it was less significant than the struggle
which he waged, when he was at the height
of his political power, against the menace of
class cleavage.

It is necessary briefly to recall the economic and social conditions in the country
at the time he succeeded to the Presidency.
A few years of prosperity had succeeded a
long period of financial depression, of panics,
"hard times," industrial disturbances, un-
employment, want. The rapid development

of the country during the years immediately
following the Civil War had resulted in the
concentration of enormous financial power in
the hands of a comparatively small number
of men. Vast stretches of country had been
opened to settlement and agriculture. Trade
had expanded; the rich had grown very rich,
but all their countrymen had, through their
prosperity, prospered in turn. Those who
failed to make a living in the cities turned to
the open West. But gradually the free land
was absorbed. Prices rose as capitalists united
to suppress competition through the creation of huge monopolies; changing adminis-
trations in Washington brought constantly
changing tariff laws and financial policies;
the "trusts" throve, but the laboring man
suffered in an unwholesome alternation of "a
full dinner-pail" and hunger; the prices of
farm products fell so low that farmers despaired. Armies of the unemployed under
various names were formed to march on
Washington and demand redress. There was
a violent strike in Chicago; another among

the steel-workers in Pennsylvania. Agitators arose, preaching economic heresies, and gathered millions of followers, especially in the West.

An attempt to curb the "trusts" by law proved futile. The men who dominated the "trusts" proved stronger than the law. Governors, legislatures, and judges were their tools; college presidents, preachers, and the editors of the greatest newspapers in the country were their defenders and in effect their agents. Their grip on both great political parties seemed absolute.

The industrial "barons" became arrogant. Demands for better working conditions were refused; laws passed to meet the unwholesome conditions in congested cities or to curb the greed and tyranny of the employer were either never enforced or were declared unconstitutional by judges controlled by the financial interests or out of touch with actual conditions. The great mass vaguely known as "the laboring classes," the farmers and the working men in the factories, mut-

tered and protested. The government offered
no relief. The Populistic leaders in the West
appeared to be deliberately endeavoring to
array class against class. Their excesses merely served to strengthen the hold of the capitalists on the machinery of the opposing
party. At the time that Roosevelt succeeded
to the Presidency, the government of the
United States was rapidly developing into a
plutocracy, with the "haves" and the "have-
nots" sharply and sullenly divided.

Roosevelt had watched the growing cleavage with anxious eyes. The campaign of 1896
had, for the first time, made him sharply
conscious of the menace that lay in the popular unrest. During his earlier manhood
other problems had engaged his attention—
corruption, the spoils system, indifference to
the obligations of citizenship, hyphenism, foreign affairs, the national defense. There is no
indication on the records that he was acutely
aware of the social, economic, and industrial
movements which were rapidly developing to
a crisis. Apart from an early theoretical

leaning toward free trade, and an interest, which appears to have been rather casual, in current financial and tariff legislation, neither his public utterances nor his private correspondence reveal any absorption in economic problems. The events of the free-silver campaign, however, startled him into a realization of conditions which he instantly recognized were of supreme significance to the national welfare. Among a people that he thought he knew, a people he had always supposed immovably planted on the fundamental verities of American social and economic doctrine, an honorable and practical people, the descendants largely of pioneers, he saw a reckless passion unfold itself which he might have expected in the Old World, but had never imagined could manifest itself here. "It is appalling," he wrote to his sister, Mrs. Cowles, during the heat of the campaign, "to see how easy it is to influence with bitter rancor toward the well-off all those people who, whether through misfortune or misconduct, have failed in life."

Roosevelt abhorred the demagogy and self-delusion that lay behind the fight for "that species of dishonest money which its advocates euphoniously call cheap money"; the appeal to envy, to greed, to hatred of the able, the successful, the well-to-do, to all the forces that make for social disorder and national destruction. For the leaders he had only scorn and contempt, but for the individual, caught by their lures, he had deep and comprehending pity—"the honest man who, through no fault of his own, has met with crushing disaster, and who strikes at what he calls the conditions of society with the same unreasonable anger that makes a child strike at the table or door against which it has hurt itself."

Roosevelt was by nature a conservative, but he wore his conservatism with a difference. He recognized what the spokesmen of capital refused to recognize, that true conservatism demanded a just reappraisal of industrial conditions and prompt, far-reaching remedial action.

"Every wealthy corporation that perpetrates or is allowed to perpetrate a wrong," he said in his second annual message as Governor of New York, "helps to produce or inflame a condition of angry excitement against all corporations, which in its turn may in the end harm alike the honest and the dishonest agents of public service and thereby do far-reaching damage to the whole body politic. Much of the outcry against wealth, against the men who acquire wealth, and against the means by which it is acquired, is blind, unreasoning, and unjust; but in too many cases it has a basis in real abuses; and we must remember that every act of misconduct which affords any justification for this clamor is not only bad because of the wrong done but also because the justification thus given inevitably strengthens movements which are in reality profoundly antisocial and anticivic."

This message, delivered when Roosevelt had been in the governorship a year, contained the first clear statement of the social and economic issues confronting the new century. The lesson of the free silver campaign had sunk deep into his consciousness. He had learned what fertile ground justifiable discontent provided for the demagogue's sowing of dragon's teeth. He had seen with profound apprehension the first fissures of a new cleavage of sections in the economic rebellion of the West against the financial oligarchy of the East; he had seen the repellent spectre of class hatred stalking among a people whose only hope of happiness and well-being, he knew, lay in unity.

"The people cannot afford to go wrong, or to do wrong," he had said in 1896. "We know no North nor South, no East nor West. I am an American first. To all true Americans, sectional hatred and class hatred are equally abhorrent, and the most abhorrent of all is sectional hatred piled on class hatred." The prime tenet of Americanism, he insisted, was that there must be no social or economic cleavage.

"We have proved in this country," he said, speaking to his fellow countrymen of

Dutch extraction a year later, "that we are bound to have union of the sections, that we shall have no disunion among the States. Neither must there be disunion among the classes. We must make our people feel that from the highest to the lowest, each American worthy of the name feels for all Americans, and wishes to make them rise if he rises. Exactly as from Maine to Texas and Oregon we are all one people, so that no disaster can befall one part of the community without befalling the others, so also we must feel that from the top to the bottom of the social strata our welfare is bound up with that of the others."

Roosevelt recognized that the first step in preserving the national unity was to remove the more flagrant of the abuses of individualistic liberty against which the popular protest was directed. The record of his administration as President is a record of one continual and increasingly bitter struggle to persuade, and, when persuasion failed, to force the leaders of capital to face realities and to meet the growing menace of unrest before it overwhelmed them. He was convinced that the only way adequately and definitely to meet it was to make the government the most efficient possible instrument in helping the people of the United States to better themselves politically, socially, and industrially. With all his heart he believed in "real and thoroughgoing democracy," and wished to make this democracy industrial as well as political.

"If we allow great industrial organizations to exercise unregulated control of the means of production and the necessaries of life," he declared, "we deprive the Americans of to-day and of the future of industrial liberty, a right no less precious and vital than political freedom. Industrial liberty was a fruit of political liberty, and in turn has become one of its chief supports, and exactly as we stand for political democracy so we must stand for industrial democracy."

He believed in the rights of the people and therefore in national rights and in

States' rights to the degree in which they severally secured popular rights. He believed "in invoking the national power with absolute freedom for every national need," and he insisted "that the Constitution should be regarded as the greatest document ever devised by the wit of man to aid a people in exercising every power necessary for its own betterment, and not as a straitjacket cunningly fashioned to strangle growth."

The anthracite coal strike in 1902 brought the menace of unrest for an instant terrifyingly close. The miners were insistent in their demands; the operators were obdurate. Roosevelt for the first time asserted the right of the President to act as representative of the public in an industrial dispute. His point of view is to-day so universally taken for granted that it is difficult to comprehend the wrath and confusion in the ranks of the capitalists of which the newspapers of the time bear witness. The miners agreed to arbitrate, but the operators were indignant at his interference in what they regarded as their private

concern, and stood firm. Roosevelt declared
that no men and no groups of men had the
right, through a private quarrel, to imperil
the well-being and even the lives of millions
of their countrymen. But "the operators,"
said Roosevelt afterward, "were prepared to
see civil war in the country rather than back
down." They called him revolutionary, but
Roosevelt, with sure vision, insisted that it
was he who was the conservative and they
who were the radicals.

"May Heaven preserve me," he exclaimed
in a letter to his sister after the fight was won,
"from ever again dealing with so wooden-
headed a set, when I wish to preserve their
interests!"

He saw clearly what the operators would
not see, that the labor problem had entered
upon a new phase; that the growth of industry necessitated a new approach to the
questions affecting it; that the public was in
no mood to suffer for the inability of capitalists to recognize the parity of human rights
with the rights of property; and that in a

winter of coal famine lay the possible be-
ginnings of irreparable discontent.

Sharply conscious of the spectre of a vir-
tual oligarchical despotism looming on the
one hand, and the spectre of civil war and
revolution rising darkly on the other, Roosevelt proceeded to snatch capital and labor
alike back from the extremes toward which
both were drifting. With the Northern Se-
curities suit, he revitalized the Sherman Anti-
Trust Act; under it he brought suit against
other offending corporations. By successive
acts he remedied in part the anomaly by
which the great corporations had hitherto
escaped the jurisdiction alike of State and
federal authority. With the purpose of
breaking the strangle-hold of a small minority
on the sources of wealth which should be open
to the honest endeavors of all the people,
he embraced the policy of conservation.
Under the free individualism of the past the
national resources had been recklessly ex-
ploited with no thought of the needs of coming generations. The timber-lands had largely

been stripped bare; the control of the nation's water-power had to a great extent passed into private hands; the public grazing-lands were yielding vast profits to the sheep owners and cattle owners, but none to the people as a whole to whom they belonged; the wealth in minerals and oil in the public domain was yielding enormous dividends to a few and none whatever to the government which was the people's trustee.

"The function of our government," he insisted, "is to insure to all its citizens, now and hereafter, their rights of life, liberty, and the pursuit of happiness. If we of this generation destroy the resources from which our children would otherwise derive their livelihood, we reduce the capacity of our land to support a population, and so either degrade the standard of living or deprive the coming generations of their right to live on this continent."

It was Roosevelt's policy to promote local development of the public lands by the settlement of home makers "to serve all the people legitimately and openly, instead of permitting the lands to be converted, illegitimately and under cover, to the private benefit of a few"; and to use the public forests and the nation's water power for the permanent public good, instead of merely for temporary private gain. Under his administration vast stretches of land rich in timber, coal, minerals, and oil were withdrawn from private exploitation.

Here, too, the opposition which developed was powerful and unrelenting. The intrenched forces of special privilege fought him with all their cohorts, believing sincerely that, in insisting on the limitations of individualistic enterprise, he was shaking the foundations of the social structure and undermining the institution of private property. He did not permit their vehemence to shake him in his determination that fundamental justice must and should be done. Day after day, month after month, in the White House and on long journeys over the country he preached the gospel of the real conservatism.

"Ours is a government of liberty by,

through, and under the law," he said at Spo-
kane in 1903. "No man is above it and no
man is below it. The crime of cunning, the
crime of greed, the crime of violence, are all
equally crimes, and against them all alike
the law must set its face. This is not and
never shall be a government either of plutocracy or of a mob. It is, it has been, and it
will be a government of the people; including
alike the people of great wealth, of moderate
wealth, the people who employ others, the
people who are employed, the wage-worker,
the lawyer, the mechanic, the banker, the
farmer; including them all, protecting each
and every one if he acts decently and squarely, and discriminating against any one of
them, no matter from what class he comes, if
he does not act squarely and fairly, if he does
not obey the law. While all people are foolish
if they violate or rail against the law—
wicked as well as foolish, but all foolish—yet
the most foolish man in this Republic is the
man of wealth who complains because the
law is administered with impartial justice

against or for him. His folly is greater than the folly of any other man who so complains; for he lives and moves and has his being because the law does in fact protect him and his property.

"We have the right to ask every decent American citizen to rally to the support of the law if it is ever broken against the interest of the rich man; and we have the same right to ask that rich man cheerfully and gladly to acquiesce in the enforcement against his seeming interest of the law, if it is the law. Incidentally, whether he acquiesces or not, the law will be enforced; and this whoever he may be, great or small, and at whichever end of the social scale he may be."

He insisted on strict and impartial enforcement of the law as President as he had insisted on it as Civil Service Commissioner, as Police Commissioner, and as Governor, in the first place because he recognized that to do otherwise was to undermine all respect for law; and, in the second place, because he saw with unfaltering vision that to discriminate in favor of any special interest, whether that special interest was capital or labor, was to strengthen the belief, loudly proclaimed by the discontented elements in the nation, that might made right, that God was on the side that had the heaviest battalions and that the only way to secure what one group or another desired was by force. To permit such a belief to gain credence was, he knew, to fortify those who were seeking to array class against class and to play into the hands of those others who were working for the overthrow of all orderly government.

"I ask that we see to it in our country that the line of division in the deeper matters of our citizenship be drawn, never between section and section, never between creed and creed, never, thrice never, between class and class, but that the line be drawn on the line of conduct, cutting through sections, cutting through creeds, cutting through classes; the line that divides the honest from the dishonest, the line that divides good citizenship from bad citizenship, the line that declares a man a good citizen only if, and always if, he acts in accordance with the immutable law of righteousness, which has been the same from the beginning of history to the present moment and which will be the same from now until the end of recorded time."

Only by enforcing the law without regard to persons or special interests, he knew, could the unity of the American people be preserved.

XI

HE was abused as a destroyer and a demagogue. Newspapers and politicians railed at him as a revolutionary, a socialist, a crazy man, a megalomaniac running amuck, accusing him of creating the very class cleavage which he was laboring to prevent. But the suggestion of a labor leader that he was on the side of labor against capital, he met with a sharp rebuke. "While I am President, the White House door will swing as easily for the laboring man as for the capitalist—and no easier."

The position he took as President was the same position he had taken in the earliest period of his political life when, in voting against a bill in the New York Legislature of 1883, forbidding convict labor, he said in the course of a hitherto unpublished speech:

"I have never said that I claimed to represent Labor, and that I would go as far as I could and do all I could for the working man. I represent neither Capital nor Labor; I represent every American citizen be he laborer or be he capitalist. I do not claim to know more than they do what the working men of this State desire. I can only say that I will try to do them justice as I have tried to do all other classes justice; or, to speak more properly, according to my lights I will strive to mete an equal measure of justice to every citizen of this State, no matter what his occupation or his nationality."

As President, he declared again with the same emphasis that he was no less the friend of capital than of labor. It was his concern to give a "square deal" to both, "no more and no less."

It was a shock to him when he discovered that a "square deal" was wanted by certain elements on the one side as little as it was wanted by certain elements on the other. What both wanted was not justice, but special privilege. Each regarded the application of justice to the other as something less than the punishment due; but justice applied to itself, each vociferously declared, was class legislation of the most abominable description.

Roosevelt was besieged in the White House no less by labor leaders than by the heads of the great corporations. He pointed out to them that he must govern his actions by the law of the land, which he was sworn to administer, and which differentiated any case in which the United States was a party from all other cases whatsoever. Laws enacted for the benefit of the whole people could not and must not be construed as permitting discrimination against some of the people.

"I am President of all the people of the United States, without regard to creed, color, birthplace, occupation, or social condition. My aim is to do equal and exact justice as among them all."

He refused to regard the protest of a committee of the Federation of Labor against the reinstatement of an employee of the Government Printing Office who had been dismissed by the Public Printer following his expulsion from his union.

"In the employment and dismissal of men in the government service," he declared, "I can no more recognize the fact that a man does or does not belong to a union as being for or against him than I can recognize the fact that he is a Protestant or a Catholic, a Jew or a Gentile as being for or against him."

In the turmoil in the press concerning Roosevelt's endeavor to force capital into the straight and narrow path, his similar efforts in regard to labor were sometimes lost sight of; and only the more penetrating and open-minded of the capitalists were willing to admit that the shots were not all falling in one camp.

With all his power he strove both by administrative and legislative action "to advance the cause of labor, to protect it from unjust aggression and secure to it its legitimate rights." On the other hand, he insisted that when any labor union sought improper ends, or sought to achieve proper ends by improper methods, public servants who were conscious of their responsibility must oppose the wrong-doing as resolutely as they would oppose the wrong-doing of any great corporation.

"I will do everything in my power for the wage workers of the country *except to do what is wrong.* I will do wrong for no man; and with all the force in my power I solemnly warn the laboring men of the country that any public man who advocates doing wrong in their interest cannot be trusted by them."

Violence, brutality or corruption he would no more tolerate on the part of labor than on the part of capital. Rule by the mob, he de-

clared, was no better than rule by the rich.
The preachers and apostles of violence and
disorder, he insisted, had done as much to
discredit the labor movement as the worst
speculative financiers or the most unscrupu-
lous employers of labor had done to discredit
honest capitalists and fair-dealing business
men.

"They have adopted practices which cut
them off from those who lead this legitimate
movement. In every way I shall support the
law-abiding and upright representatives of
labor; and in no way can I better support
them than by drawing the sharpest possible
line between them, on the one hand, and
on the other hand those preachers of violence
who are themselves the worst foes of the
honest laboring man."

XII

THE letter in which Roosevelt denounced
a prominent financier and certain extremist
labor leaders alike as "undesirable citizens,"
brought him fierce denunciation from both

camps. But even while he was hotly condemning the extremists, he was endeavoring with all the persuasive power which he possessed to bring the reasonable, the progressive, the high-minded, and the unselfish elements in both groups, irrespective of party affiliations, to some sound basis of common effort, which would remove friction and would bring both groups once more into accordance with the fundamental principles of American institutions, fair-handed justice, and equal opportunity to all. He insisted that employer and employed alike must show not merely insistence each upon his own rights, but also regard for the rights of others, and a full acknowledgment of the interests of the third party—the public. There must be no yielding to wrong on either side; but there must be not only desire to do right but a willingness each to try to understand the view-point of his fellow, with whom, for weal or for woe, his own fortunes were indissolubly bound.

He begged for mutual understanding, for the understanding which he himself had won by mingling with men and women of all sections and races and classes and creeds, talking with them, working with them, learning their needs, their sufferings, their aspirations.

"I firmly believe in my countrymen," he said, speaking before the Brotherhood of Locomotive Engineers in Chattanooga in 1902, "and, therefore, I believe that the chief thing necessary in order that they will work together is that they shall know one another —that the Northerner shall know the Southerner, and the man of one occupation know the man of another occupation; the man who works in one walk of life know the man who works in another walk of life, so that we may realize that the things which divide us are superficial, are unimportant, and that we are, and must ever be, knit together into one indissoluble mass by our common American brotherhood."

He had no illusions concerning the magnitude of the problems with which he was grappling. He recognized fully and frankly that there were endless difficulties involved in any effort to secure "a healthy, self-respecting and mutually sympathetic attitude" between employer and employee, between capitalist and wage worker and to work out "a system or rule of conduct, whether with or without the help of the lawgiver, which shall minimize that jarring and clashing of interests in the industrial world which causes so much individual irritation and suffering and which at times threatens baleful consequences to large portions of the body politic." All phases of the labor problem, he had found, presented thorny edges. But he insisted that there was a root principle in accordance with which progress was possible.

"We can get justice and right dealing," he declared, "only if we put as of paramount importance the principle of treating a man on his worth as a man rather than with reference to his social position, his occupation, or the class to which he belongs."

There was, he knew, no "patent remedy" for the solution of the problems which confronted the industrial world. They could be solved only if all parties concerned brought to their solution a broad sympathy and a desire for mutual understanding and strove to keep out of the solution "some of the most familiar and most undesirable of the traits to which mankind has owed untold degradation and suffering throughout the ages. Arrogance, suspicion, brutal envy of the well-to-do, brutal indifference toward those who are not well-to-do, the hard refusal to consider the rights of others, the foolish refusal to consider the limits of beneficent action, the base appeal to the spirit of selfish greed, whether it take the form of plunder of the fortunate or of oppression of the unfortunate —from these and from all kindred vices this nation must be kept free if it is to remain in its present position in the forefront of the peoples of mankind."

In speech after speech he endeavored to create a closer understanding by pointing out in simple terms that "the colonel's lady and Judy O'Grady are sisters under the skin."

"Now and then," he would say, "we meet well-meaning people who have a genuine horror and dread of all rich men and think of them as being set apart by peculiar vice and iniquity. Now and then we meet equally well-meaning rich men who have an equally irrational dread of those whom they style 'labor leaders.' In each case I think the hostility is in large part due to a want of sympathy caused by complete ignorance of the men who arouse such distrust or anger. As a matter of fact, if we take a given number of men of large fortune and a like number of wage workers, we find that in their essential human nature they are all alike. In each group we find men as wise and as foolish, as good and as bad as in the other group."

Men being as they are, similarly constituted whatever brand they wear or whatever banner they fly, the transgressions of one group or the other should be regarded rather "as a wrong to be remedied than as a wrong to be avenged."

"We ought not to tolerate wrong. It is a

sign of weakness, and in its ultimate effects weakness is often quite as bad as wickedness. But in putting a stop to the wrong, we should, so far as possible, avoid getting into an attitude of vindictive hatred toward the wrong-doer."

He recognized that there were two kinds of wrong involved, the wrong that was due to moral transgression and the wrong due to the economic and social conditions under which the wrong-doer found himself. In the latter case, he insisted, it was necessary to apply the remedy, but it was neither just nor far-sighted to exact revenge.

"We are knit together in ties of brother-hood," he declared, and brothers, living under the same roof, could not afford to be at odds.

Persistently, day in, day out, he emphasized the essential need for unity. Decade by decade, he insisted, it was becoming more necessary for the people, without sacrificing their individual independence, to recognize more effectively their mutual interdependence and the duty of safeguarding the interest of each in the ultimate interest of all; more necessary to show "by deeds and words our knowledge that in such a government as ours each of us must be in very truth his brother's keeper." The fundamental condition of success in self-government, he insisted, was unity, "standing shoulder to shoulder, working in association, by organization, each working for all, and yet remembering that we need each so to shape things that each man can develop to best advantage all the forces and powers at his command."

He was accused loudly of being a "socialist," a "paternalist." His answer was unequivocal.

"We have inherited and developed a superbly self-reliant individualism in this country. I most earnestly hope that it will not be lost, that it will never be exchanged for a deadening socialism. The only permanently beneficial way in which to help any one is to help him to help himself; if either private

charity or governmental action or any form
of social expression destroys the individual's
power of self-help, the greatest possible wrong
is really done to the individual."

There was scarcely a speech which he delivered as President in which he did not insist that the essential element in all progress
was not legislation, but character. He believed heartily in the value of legislation to
curb reckless individualism and to give the
people the power over their own government
which enlightened democratic thought demanded; no one in the history of the nation
indeed ever fought harder than he to secure
such legislation. But he had no illusions concerning its limitations and he took every occasion to impress these limitations on the
public mind. He was always warning the
public against "panaceas," against too simple
a faith in the efficacy of mere legislation.
Laws are important, he insists, new laws
from time to time are needed, wise laws and
their honest enforcement can do much to
break down old tyrannies and to open fresh

opportunities, but, in the long run, it is the possession of the elemental virtues which determines whether an individual or a nation shall move forward and live, or shall disintegrate and perish—honesty, strength, courage, hardihood, "steady adherence to duty in the teeth of difficulty, in the teeth of discouragement, and even disaster," the desire to do justice and the insistence that justice be done; self-restraint, the power of self-mastery, "the capacity to work for and with others as well as for oneself, the power of giving to others the love which each of us must bear for his neighbor, if we are to make our civilization really great"; the pioneering mind, the spirit of "on and on." Unless the average man and woman, he declares again and again, possess and practise the elemental virtues, the wisest laws will be worse than futile in establishing national well-being. Unless the individual citizen is honest, fearless, and intelligent, and is willing to "carry his own weight," no legislation can make him anything except a failure and a public burden.

Roosevelt's emphasis on the individual and his constant insistence that the essential element in progress is the moral and spiritual growth of each individual citizen, was a factor whose importance cannot be disregarded in any study of his influence on the American mind. Apart from its value as sound morality, this doctrine, whose platitudinous nature Roosevelt's critics lamented, had a significant bearing on Roosevelt's fight for an undivided America. It discouraged group action; with its emphasis on the supreme importance of character, it minimized by direct implication the value of mere brute force either political or physical. The high seriousness with which Roosevelt was denounced during his lifetime as an "apostle of force" reveals how little even the most discussed man of his time may be really understood. To Roosevelt the foundation of the nation and the basis of all progress was character. In his insistence on dividing men only on lines of conduct, he cut across the artificial boundaries that separated section from section, sect from sect, race from race, class from class, and united Northerner and Southerner, Protestant and Catholic, Gentile and Jew, foreign-born and native-born, capitalist and laborer, white and black, on the basis of their common Americanism.

Roosevelt's conviction — so firmly implanted in him that it was a part of his nature—that any permanent solution of the nation's social and industrial problems depended ultimately on the intelligence and righteousness of the individual, did not blind him to the immediate need of curbing the free individualism of the earlier days. The vast growth of industries and of cities had, he declared, created situations with which the individual could no longer cope alone. A farmer employing a hired man was one thing; a great corporation employing a hundred thousand hired men was another. It was not possible, he insisted, to trust the welfare of the people only to the "unbridled individual initiative" of each unit of the population working as that unit willed. Laws were needed for the protec-

tion of children which were unnecessary in
the nation's youth; laws were needed for the
control of corporations which were not needed
when fortunes were small and business re-
stricted; laws were needed for the adjustment
of labor conditions which were not needed
when the bulk of the people lived on farms.
He had no intention, he declared, of trying
to work "for the impossible and undesirable
end of giving to the lazy, the thriftless, the
weak, and the vicious the reward that belongs to, and in the long run can only come
to, the hard working, the thrifty, the resolute,
and the honest." But he insisted that the
necessary struggle in life be carried on under
genuinely democratic conditions; that, so far
as human action could safely provide it, there
should be an approximately fair start; that
there should be no oppression of the weak,
and that no man should be permitted to acquire or to use a vast fortune by methods that
were tortuous and dishonest.

He pointed out that there was a middle
course between unrestricted individualism

and the socialistic panacea which would destroy all individualism. "In any great movement, such as that in which we are engaged, nothing is more necessary than sanity, than the refusal to be led into extremes by the advocates of the ultra course on either side. Those professed friends of liberty who champion license are the worst foes of liberty and tend by the reaction their violence causes to throw the government back into the hands of the men who champion corruption and tyranny in the name of order."

He took the middle ground and inevitably became the target for the extremists, the "lunatic fringe," of both groups. But he knew that he was right, and let the storm rage, for he knew that industrial peace and with it unity and the opportunity for that pursuit of happiness the Declaration declares man's "inalienable right" could be made a reality only by the stern persistence on the part of the government in doing even-handed, unprejudiced justice to rich and poor alike.

XIII

As Roosevelt's administration drew to a close the struggle became increasingly bitter. A severe panic in the summer of 1907, due to overinflation and overspeculation, accentuated the vindictiveness of the opposition. The panic was due, in part at least, to causes operative alike on the bourses of London, Paris, and Berlin, for the disturbance was world-wide; but in the New York Stock Exchange it was particularly severe, and frightened bank presidents and clamorous depositors united in placing the responsibility on Roosevelt's shoulders. Roosevelt accepted it with a certain grim satisfaction. "I am responsible for turning on the light," he declared. "I am not responsible for what the light reveals."

"It may well be," he said in the course of an address that summer, "that the determination of the government (in which, gentlemen, it will not waver) to punish certain malefactors of great wealth, has been responsible for something of the trouble; at least to the extent of having caused these men to combine to bring about as much financial stress as possible, in order to discredit the policy of the government and thereby secure a reversal of that policy, so that they may enjoy unmolested the fruits of their own evil-doing. That they have misled many good people into believing that there should be such reversal of policy is possible. If so, I am sorry; but it will not alter my attitude.

"Once for all let me say that so far as I am concerned, and for the eighteen months of my Presidency that remain, there will be no change in the policy we have steadily pursued, no let up in the effort to secure the honest observance of the law; *for I regard this contest as one to determine who shall rule this free country*—the people through their governmental agents, or a few ruthless and domineering men whose wealth makes them peculiarly formidable because they hide behind the breastworks of corporate organization. I wish there to be no mistake on this point; it is idle to ask me not to prosecute criminals, rich or poor."

This speech marks the beginning of a new phase of the struggle in which Roosevelt was engaged. In it he states nakedly for the first time the fundamental issues at stake, whether the law should be interpreted, as it had too often been interpreted in the past, by the rich man for the benefit of the rich man or whether it should be interpreted by honest servants of the government for the benefit of the whole people; whether in brief a small plutocratic group should hold the vast majority in economic and political subjection, or, as the Constitution intended, the whole people, irrespective of wealth or social position, should govern the nation.

He saw with clear vision that the tyranny of a minority must inevitably in turn bring the equally disastrous tyranny of the mob. He pointed to the example of Rome and the example of France. The Roman Republic had fallen largely because the political life of the nation had become split between two camps,

one containing the rich who wished to exploit
the poor, and the other the poor who wished
to plunder the rich; and the public man who
was for the moment successful had in conse-
quence tended to be either a violent reactionary or a violent demagogue. In France,
likewise, he pointed out, the people had split
into two sharply defined classes, one of unreasonable conservatism, the other of unreasonable radicalism. "Had pre-Revolu-
tionary France listened to men like Turgot,
and backed them up," he declared, "all would
have gone well. But the beneficiaries of privilege, the Bourbon reactionaries, the short-
sighted ultraconservatives, turned down Turgot; and then found that instead of him
they had obtained Robespierre. They gained
twenty years' freedom from all restraint and
reform at the cost of the whirlwind of the red
terror; and in their turn the unbridled extremists of the terror induced a blind reaction; and so, with convulsion and oscillation
from one extreme to another, with alterna-
tions of violent radicalism and violent Bour-

bonism, the French people went through misery toward a shattered goal. May we profit by the experience of our brother republicans across the water, and go forward steadily, avoiding all wild extremes; and may our ultraconservatives remember that the rule of the Bourbons brought on the Revolution, and may our would-be revolutionaries remember that no Bourbon was ever such a dangerous enemy of the people and of freedom as the professed friend of both, Robespierre. There is no danger of a revolution in this country; but there is grave discontent and unrest, and in order to remove them there is need of all the wisdom and probity and deep-seated faith in and ·purpose to uplift humanity we have at our command."

The American people, he pointed out, had achieved democracy in politics just because they had hitherto been able to steer a middle course between the rule of the mob and the rule of the dictator, and could achieve industrial democracy only by steering a similar middle course "between the extreme individualist and the socialist, between the demagogue who attacks all wealth and who can see no wrong done anywhere unless it is perpetrated by a man of wealth, and the apologist for the plutocracy who rails against so much as a restatement of the eighth commandment upon the ground that it will 'hurt business.'"

He never despaired of the outcome. He believed implicitly in the future of the nation, believing as he no less implicitly did that the average American citizen would no more tolerate government by a mob than he would tolerate government by a plutocracy.

He recalled the teachings and the practice of Lincoln: "Oppose the dangerous extremes; stand on middle ground; hold the ship steady and level; to desert such ground . . . is to be less than a man—less than an American."

He was accused of being a radical. He pointed out that Lincoln had been a great radical—"of course a wise and cautious radical—otherwise he could have done nothing for the forward movement. But he was the

efficient leader of this forward movement."
Lincoln, too, he emphasized, had believed in
a constructive system which, while guarding
the rights of capital, should see that the benefits were as widely diffused as possible and
that all artificial obstacles to a fair start in
the world and to financial democracy were
done away with. "From all his record it is
safe to say that if Lincoln had lived to deal
with our complicated social and industrial
problems he would have furnished a wisely
conservative leadership; but he would have
led in the radical direction."

"I am popular because I am trusted," he
said to his aide, Captain Butt, "and I believe
my policies to be best for all classes. If ever
the unidentified class in this country feel that
the legislative class is not to be relied upon,
then may wealth and culture really expect
trouble. In this country we have got to play
the game squarely, for if we don't we will not
be allowed to play it at all. The people are
too well educated to be fooled."

A few months before his death he stated in

unforgetable words the fundamental problem
of a self-governing people:

"From the days when civilized man first
began to strive for self-government and democracy, success in this effort has depended
primarily upon the ability to steer clear of
extremes. For almost its entire length the
course lies between Scylla and Charybdis; and
the heated extremists who insist upon avoiding only one gulf of destruction invariably
land in the other—and then take refuge in the
meagre consolation afforded by denouncing
as 'inconsistent' the pilot who strives to avoid
both. Throughout past history Liberty has
always walked between the twin terrors of
Tyranny and Anarchy. They have stalked
like wolves beside her, with murder in their
red eyes, ever ready to tear each other's
throats, but ever more ready to rend in sun-
der Liberty herself. Always in the past there
has been a monotonously recurrent cycle in
the history of free states; Liberty has supplanted Tyranny, has gradually been supplanted by Anarchy, and has then seen the

insupportable Anarchy finally overthrown and Tyranny re-established. Anarchy is always and everywhere the handmaiden of Tyranny and Liberty's deadliest foe. No people can permanently remain free unless it possesses the stern self-control and resolution necessary to put down anarchy. Order without liberty and liberty without order are equally destructive; special privilege for the few and special privilege for the many are alike profoundly anti-social."

Through the storm and the confusion of counsel and appeal that beat about his administration, he pursued his course with sure vision and single-minded purpose. To him there was only one great issue before the country, whether there should be government by class or government by all; and only one great aim before the Administration, to which all other minor purposes were directed; to make the wealth and power of the nation available to every American who had the energy to claim his share.

The building of the Panama Canal; the conservation of the natural resources of coal and oil and timber and mineral wealth; the betterment of country life; the improvement of the national waterways; reclamation; the control of monopolies; the prohibition of political contributions from corporations; railroad-rate control—all, he declared, were expressions of one great purpose. "The great anthracite coal strike was settled, and the pressing danger of a coal famine averted, because we recognized that the control of a public necessity involves a duty to the people, and that public intervention in the affairs of a public-service corporation is neither to be resented as usurpation nor permitted as a privilege by the corporations, but on the contrary to be accepted as a duty and exercised as a right by the Government in the interest of all the people. The efficiency of the army and the navy has been increased so that our people may follow in peace the great work of making this country a better place for Americans to live in, and our navy was sent round the world for the same ultimate purpose. All the acts taken by the Government during the last seven years, and all the policies now being pursued by the Government, fit in as parts of a consistent whole . . . integral parts of the same attempt, the attempt to enthrone justice and righteousness, to secure freedom of opportunity to all of our citizens, now and hereafter, and to set the ultimate interest of all of us above the temporary interest of any individual, class, or group."

At bottom, his fight was a fight to preserve the national unity.

XIV

Roosevelt retired from the Presidency in 1909. When he returned to America after a year's hunting in Africa, he found the forces whose control of the machinery of government he had broken, reasserting their old power; and the old alliance of crooked business and crooked politics clutching at the helm from which he had sternly thrust it during the years of his administration. He toured the country, speaking on the "new nationalism," which must supplant the old unfettered individualism. Wherever he went he found a deep unrest, a growing bitterness, a sense that the dream of the fathers was fading and that the institutions of the fathers remained a reality only in their outward forms. In speech after speech he made clear how the old institutions could and should be adapted to the new conditions, made real again, revitalized. As before, he demanded justice for the honest capitalist as for the honest working man. The only cleavage he would admit was the cleavage between right and wrong, between the law-abiding majority and the law-defying few.

He fought the fight for national solidarity and the right of the people to control their own destinies with a fiery passion which gave his words the large sweep and universality of Old Testament prophecy.

"Our country—this great republic—means nothing unless it means the triumph of a real democracy, the triumph of popular government," he declared at Ossawatomie, "and, in the long run, of an economic system under which each man shall be guaranteed the opportunity to show the best that there is in him. That is why the history of America is now the central feature of the history of the world; for the world has set its face hopefully toward our democracy; and, oh, my fellow citizens, each one of you carries on your shoulders not only the burden of doing well for the sake of your own country, but the burden of doing well and of seeing that this nation does well for the sake of mankind. We cannot afford weakly to blind ourselves to the actual conflict which faces us to-day. The issue is joined, and we must fight or fall."

The issue to him was clear, whether the destinies of the people should be determined by the people themselves or by beneficiaries of special privilege who twisted the methods of free government into machinery for defeating the popular will.

"Exactly as the special interests of cotton and slavery threatened our political integrity before the Civil War, so now the great special business interests too often control and corrupt the men and methods of government for their own profit. We must drive the special interests out of politics. . . . Every special interest is entitled to justice, but not one is entitled to a vote in Congress, to a voice on the bench, or to representation in any public office. The Constitution guarantees protection to property, and we must make that promise good. But it does not give the right of suffrage to any corporation. We are face to face with new conceptions of the relations of property to human welfare, chiefly because certain advocates of the rights of property as against the rights of men have been pushing their claims too far. The man who wrongly holds that every human right is secondary to his profit must now give way to the advocate of human welfare, who rightly maintains that every man holds his property subject to the general right of the community to regulate its use to whatever degree the public welfare may require it. . . . The new nationalism puts the national need before sectional or personal advantage."

His opponents called him a demagogue and leader of the mob. "Well," he said, with his familiar grin, addressing a typical crowd of substantial Westerners, "you are the mob."

Reactionaries, attacking him for his criticism of the judiciary, spoke apprehensively of "the tyranny of the majority." He promptly took up the challenge:

"I have scant patience with this talk of the tyranny of the majority," he declared. "Whenever there is tyranny of the majority, I shall protest against it with all my heart and soul. But we are to-day suffering from the tyranny of minorities. It is a small minority that is grabbing our coal deposits, our water-powers, and our harbor fronts. A small minority is battening on the sale of adulterated foods and drugs. It is a small minority that lies behind monopolies and trusts. It is a small minority that stands behind the present law of master and servant, the sweatshops, and the whole calendar of social and industrial injustice. It is a small minority that is to-day using our convention system to defeat the will of a majority of the people in the choice of delegates. The only tyrannies from which men, women, and children are suffering in real life are the tyrannies of minorities."

The Progressive campaign of 1912 was the culmination of Roosevelt's fight for a return to true popular government against the rule of the privileged few, the struggle for national solidarity against social and economic cleavage. In the course of that bitterly contested campaign he rose to heights of inspiration and fervor which make the speeches of his Presidential period, vigorous and flashing as many of them were, seem by contrast almost colorless. A deep passion possessed him and came to utterance in words of vibrant splendor.

"Our task as Americans is to strive for social and industrial justice, achieved through the genuine rule of the people. This is our end, our purpose. The methods for achieving the end are merely expedients, to be finally accepted or rejected according as actual experience shows that they work well or ill. But in our hearts we must have this lofty purpose, and we must strive for it in all earnestness and sincerity, or our work will come to nothing.

"We, here in America, hold in our hands the hope of the world, the fate of the coming years; and shame and disgrace will be ours if in our eyes the light of high resolve is dimmed, if we trail in the dust the golden hopes of men. If on this new continent we merely build another country of great but unjustly divided material prosperity, we shall have done nothing; and we shall do as little if we merely set the greed of envy against the greed of arrogance, and thereby destroy the material well-being of all of us. To turn this Government either into government by a plutocracy or government by a mob would be to repeat on a larger scale the lamentable failures of the world that is dead. We stand against all tyranny, by the few or by the many. We stand for the rule of the many in the interest of all of us, for the rule of the many in a spirit of courage, of common sense, of high purpose, above all in a spirit of kindly justice toward every man and every woman. . . . The worth of our great experiment depends upon its being in good faith an experiment—the first that has ever been tried in true democracy on the scale of a continent. . . . Surely this is a noble ideal, an ideal for which it is worth while to strive, an ideal for which at need it is worth while to sacrifice much; for our ideal is the rule of all the people in a spirit of friendliest brotherhood toward each and every one of the people."

In those words, Roosevelt stated the aims of a decade's struggle against the intrenched forces of privilege. His opponents saw, or pretended to see, only that he was "unsettling business" and smashing precedents which, to those who profited by them, had the sanctity of manna from on high. But Roosevelt knew that the question went deeper than any temporary movement of financial prosperity or adversity. The American principle of government which Washington had established, which Lincoln had preserved and strengthened, was involved. In a nation in which either the capitalist or the working man exercised domination over the other and over the rest of the people the principles of the Constitution could not survive. Government by a class—by any class—for a benefit of that class was the negation of government of the people, by the people, for the people, the whole people.

At every point Roosevelt's fight for national unity was a fight for the perpetuation of American institutions.

It was inexplicable to him why his opponents failed to see that in working for the welfare of all he was maintaining their welfare in the only way in which that welfare could be permanently maintained. He was so firmly convinced that the course he had followed was the course which the highest interests of the country demanded, that he bore the taunts and derision of his enemies with untroubled spirit. He fought with superb vigor and flashing humor, a hard-hitting fighter in a hard-hitting world; and in his heart there was the exaltation of one who gives himself without reserve to a cause which is worthy of a strong man's devotion. "The leader for the time being," he said, "is but an instrument, to be used until broken and then to be cast aside; and if he is worth his salt he will care no more when he is broken than a soldier cares when he is sent where his life is forfeit in order that the victory may be won. In the long fight for righteousness the watchword for all of us is spend and be spent. It is of little matter whether any one man fails or succeeds; but the cause shall not fail, for it is the cause of mankind."

Roosevelt went down to apparent defeat; the instrument was broken and for the moment cast aside; the party he had founded died as domestic issues faded from sight in the presence of the even more elemental issues

presented by the war in Europe. But the
cause for which Roosevelt fought did not go
down to defeat. The forces which for generations had controlled the dominant party were
routed; the candidate who was elected was
able, because of the issues which Roosevelt
had raised and made paramount, to repudi-
ate the sinister elements which had exercised
similar control over the Democratic party;
and in the first administration of Woodrow
Wilson many of the reforms for which Roosevelt and the forces he led had battled became
the law of the land. The passage of time
has established the policies which he first
presented and fought for. The position he
took at the time of the coal strike, that the
President had a right as the representative
of the public to interfere in industrial dis-
putes affecting large numbers of the people,
has come to be accepted as a matter of course.
His doctrine of the necessary limitation of
individual or corporate enterprise by federal
control has become part of the national tradition. His conservation policy, despite, or

perhaps because of, the sabotage of corrupt or complacent officials, has come gradually to win the impassioned and determined support of all except an insignificant and interested minority.

The fight for national unity against social cleavage is not ended; the struggle for the reality against the sham of popular government is not won, and as long as human beings are moved by greed and the hunger for power, will not at any time be permanently won. The right to life, liberty, and the pursuit of happiness must be ardently claimed and valiantly fought for by each generation in turn. But because Roosevelt lived and worked and preached and struggled and stormed the citadel, the fight for the generations to come will be an easier fight, for they will have Roosevelt's words to guide them and Roosevelt's name for a rallying cry and a symbol.

XV

ROOSEVELT'S struggles against sectional cleavage, against religious cleavage, against race cleavage, against social and economic cleavage were different phases of the one great struggle which he waged all his life for national unity. That struggle was, it is worth repeating, fundamentally a struggle for the very existence of the Republic.

"Strive for unity," he pleaded. "As a people we must be united. If we are not united we shall slip into the gulf of measureless disaster."

His fight for national preparedness and his prodigious effort to wake a slumbering people to a sense of the peril which confronted it and of the high, hard duty that peril entailed, were to him struggles in which failure meant the loss of all that the people's endeavors for national solidarity and well-being had won.

"It is of no use talking about reform and social justice and equality of industrial opportunity inside of a nation," he insisted, "unless that nation can protect itself from outside attack. It is not worth while bothering about any social or industrial problem in the United States unless the United States is willing to train itself, to fit itself, so that it can be sure that its own people will have the say-so in the settlement of these problems, and not some nation of alien invaders and oppressors."

In this assertion of a grim truth, he was repeating in different words the reason he had given in his final message to Congress for his efforts in behalf of the national defense: "So that our people may follow in peace the great work of making this country a better place for Americans to live in."

Unity and defense, he insisted, were interrelated; without defense, unity and all its benefits were at the mercy of any strong despoiler; without unity, without "national solidarity there can be no real efficiency in either peace or war." "If we are not all of us Americans," he declared, "we won't have any nation."

The democratic ideal itself was at stake. "For democracy will assuredly go down if it once be shown that it is incompatible with national security. The law of self-preservation is the primary law for nations as for individuals. If a nation cannot protect itself under a democratic form of government, then it will either die or evolve a new form of government."

To him preparedness was more than the making of soldiers and guns; discipline was needed and guns were needed—none made that clearer than he—but the movement of which physical preparation was the obvious and immediate purpose was to him at bottom a larger thing—an effort to develop a point of view, the readiness of the soul to spend and be spent, and, scorning all differences of section or creed or race or class, to unite with all high-spirited citizens in defense of the nation's future. "The prime work for the nation at this moment," he wrote in 1915, "is to rebuild its own character. Let us find our own souls."

He spoke eloquently of "the larger Americanism"—that doctrine of national unity and national service which he had always preached. "The larger Americanism demands that we refuse to be sundered from one another along lines of class or creed or section or national origin; that we judge each American on his merits as a man; that we work for the well-being of our bodily selves, but also for the well-being of our spiritual selves, that we consider safety, but that we put honor and duty ahead of safety. Only thus shall we stand erect before the world, high of heart, the masters of our own souls, fit to be the fathers of a race of free men who shall make and shall keep this land all that it seemed to the prophetic vision of the mighty men who founded it and the mighty men who saved it."

In this last struggle of a stormy life, he rose to new heights of devotion. Old bitternesses vanished overnight; old enmities were wiped out; old alliances were severed. It mattered nothing to him whether men had fought against him in the past, or had fought at his side. If they stood for national defense and a unified people, he sought and claimed their support; if they wavered or paltered, placing secondary issues before what he regarded as the single issue which in the crisis deserved consideration, he broke with them without hesitation. With sure vision and sure tread he led the nation up the difficult path of duty.

Once more his countrymen rallied to him, united, when he died, as never before, upon a road which he had marked for them.

XVI

I HAVE indicated what appears to me to have been Roosevelt's supreme passion and aim in his public service; to help men to understand one another; to be just to one another; to admit no barriers except the barrier that separates the honest and the decent from the crooked and the foul; to have faith in American institutions and with open minds to seek ever to adjust them to ever-changing conditions and to labor to keep them pure

ROOSEVELT

and vital; to admit and to suffer no political
distinctions of section, of creed, of race, of
class; to make homogeneous a people of many
racial strains and creeds, of endlessly diverse
activities, of great individual wealth and
great poverty, of deep learning and deeper
ignorance; in the truest sense, to make such a
people a nation, and a nation such as history
has not hitherto borne record of, united not
by blood, not by common origin, not by age-
old ancestral tradition, but by a common devotion to a high ideal of government. He saw
conflicting elements and he strove to bring
them together, to the end that a consolidated,
united people might march forward to redeem
the hopes of mankind in the democratic ideal.

He was one of the world's great statesmen, using the word in its noblest sense—a
moral leader determining the course of a
people's history through words and deeds
appealing and responding to that people's
highest political ideals. Some of the tangible
results of his statesmanship I have indicated. The intangibles are these: there is,

in spite of scandals, in spite of temporary
flarebacks, an honor and an honesty in
American business life which were not there
before he applied the scourge, and which the
greatest leaders of industry have been proud
to acknowledge; there is a quickened public
conscience which will not endure corruption
in public office; there is a quickened interest
in the affairs of government, a deeper understanding of American institutions; a keener
sense of the need of individual participation
in the affairs of the city, the State, and the
nation; a profounder recognition of the glory
of national solidarity; a new understanding
of the familiar words, *Liberty and union, now
and forever, one and inseparable.* After the
leader's victories and defeats, the prophet's
adjurations, swallowed at last in silence, these
remain for younger spirits, kindled by his
fire, to develop and carry forward.

The European statesman who asked why
the American people continued to be interested in a leader who was dead, did well
to ask it. The message of Roosevelt's life

is not for his own people alone or for his own time. Wherever men throw aside the shackles of autocracy and set their feet on the difficult road that leads to democratic government, the wise and the far-seeing will turn to Roosevelt for inspiration and guidance. He understood the common man as few statesmen have understood him; he knew the enemies that beset democracy; he knew that dreams can be made into realities only by the medium of faltering, imperfect humankind and that it is only as men as individuals are lifted up that nations and peoples can be brought to higher levels. Above all, he knew that it is only by sympathy, by understanding, by an approach to the spirit of brotherhood, that liberty and lasting happiness may be secured. Not only to the hearts of his own countrymen this brother to all men calls through the dissonances of the world: *Strive for unity!*